Zbigniew Drozdowicz

Essays on European Liberalism

Development in Humanities

edited by

Zbigniew Drozdowicz
(General Editor)

and Sławomir Sztajer

Volume 13

LIT

Zbigniew Drozdowicz

Essays on European Liberalism

History and Ideology

LIT

Translated by Jan R. Kobyłecki

Typeset by Michał Staniszewski

This book is printed on acid-free paper.

Bibliographic information published by the Deutsche Nationalbibliothek
The Deutsche Nationalbibliothek lists this publication in the Deutsche Nationalbibliografie; detailed bibliographic data are available in the Internet at http://dnb.d-nb.de.

ISBN 978-3-643-90433-1

A catalogue record for this book is available from the British Library

Klosbachstr. 107
CH-8032 Zürich
Tel. +41 (0) 44-251 75 05
Fax +41 (0) 44-251 75 06
E-Mail: zuerich@lit-verlag.ch
http://www.lit-verlag.ch

LIT VERLAG Dr. W. Hopf
Berlin 2013
Fresnostr. 2
D-48159 Münster
Tel. +49 (0) 2 51-62 03 20
Fax +49 (0) 2 51-23 19 72
E-Mail: lit@lit-verlag.de
http://www.lit-verlag.de

Distribution:
In Germany: LIT Verlag Fresnostr. 2, D-48159 Münster
Tel. +49 (0) 2 51-620 32 22, Fax +49 (0) 2 51-922 60 99, E-mail: vertrieb@lit-verlag.de

In Austria: Medienlogistik Pichler-ÖBZ, e-mail: mlo@medien-logistik.at
In the UK: Global Book Marketing, e-mail: mo@centralbooks.com
In North America: International Specialized Book Services, e-mail: orders@isbs.com
e-books are available at www.litwebshop.de

Contents

Introduction

Even among people educated to an average level, the word "liberalism" evokes some associations. What they are, of course, depends on the person who speaks about it and their personal experiences of liberalism. If they are its opponents, then probably the idea of liberalism will arise as a monster with many heads, each of which destroys something. If, however, they are its supporters or liberals themselves, then maybe this will create in some people an image of a great benefactor who gives everyone something and there is still plenty left over for future generations. But more likely, the image of liberalism will appear as something with an unknown origin, without a clearly defined shape, having various internal "cracks," etc. Those people who speak positively about it, or at least without prejudice, unfortunately, do not say the same things, and the scale of the differences existing between them is so great that it can lead to despair, not only among those who would like to learn something concrete about it, but also those who undertake the task of saying something about it that is not really contradictory.[1]

Of course, I am not claiming that liberalism was and is something so uniform that we can indisputably determine the moment of its birth, its stages of maturation and transformation, the past and present forms of its manifestation, or its proximal and distal affinities. I can state, however, that with all its internal diversity and the many identifying difficulties, it is not a slogan, a "bag" which you can throw everything into and take out everything that is presently needed in the ideological or political battle. Furthermore, I claim that liberalism is neither a hymn from the past, nor the swan's contemporary song, but an ideology, philosophy and social policy that is always found in a good condition. I agree with Jerzy Szacki, that we ought to speak not about liberalism, but about many liberalisms, and that it is not possible to systematize it

[1] More on the topic of these discrepancies in defining liberalism, cf. J. Szacki, *Liberalizm po komunizmie* [Liberalism after Communism], Cracow 1994, p. 22 ff.

according to one criterion. However, this is not proof of its weakness, but its power expressed through its diversity and variety, its vitality – because we can carry out archaeological excavations "under the string," but we cannot do so with something as dynamic and lively in reacting to social events as liberalism.

In the literature, we can find different attempts to arrange and systematize it. Most often, it has been divided into "classical" liberalism and "neo-liberalism" or – which comes out to the same thing – the "old" and the "new." This division implies the belief that, over the course of its history, it has undergone at least one major breakthrough. Frequently you can also come upon this division due to the areas of social life that are clearly indicated by its presence – this point of view distinguishes, among others, political and economic liberalism. Most often, however, the basis for distinguishing it is its geographical criterion, which allows distinguishing European and American, British and continental Europe's liberalism, as well as the liberalism which occurs in different countries within our continent. Finally, we can also find such attempts as the holistic approach, in which the various criteria for its differentiation are made to complement each other.

An example of such an approach and presentation of liberalism can be the monograph by Guido de Ruggiero.[2] His approach, which I proposed, is relatively closest to it. I divide this proposed approach into "historical" (up to the World War I) and contemporary liberalism. The first, to me, seems to essentially divide it into the English, French, German and Italian. It is, however, a questionable matter whether there appeared a specific form of liberalism in other European countries, including Poland. Actually, I use the term "liberalism in Poland" and not "Polish liberalism," but I do not state that we cannot defend the validity of using the second of these terms. Further divisions are linked with changes taking place in these mentioned countries. All of them are based on the general belief that liberalism, from the moment of its birth to the present day, was not an "office philosophy," but was and is associated with concrete social realities, and these of course are different in different times and places. Thus, it is so difficult to give its overall presentation, or even to indicate what would be the interpretation of its main ideas or postulates. Nevertheless, this does not mean, of course, that such attempts are not made.

[2] Cf. G. de Ruggiero, *The History of European Liberalism*, Boston 1959.

PART I

Traditions

Chapter 1

English liberalism

1. Liberalism in the 17th and 18th centuries

The origins of English liberalism are associated with Puritanism, a religious movement entangled in political and social issues. It appeared at the end of the sixteenth century along with a wave of efforts to remove the remains of "popery" from the Church of England. As long as Elizabeth I reigned, their activities were not only tolerated but they could also count on her support in some issues, though this queen was condemned (in 1570) by Rome. The situation changed radically after James I (1603–1625), from the Scottish Stuart dynasty, took power. Not only did he try to strengthen the episcopacy (the authority of bishops in the Church of England), but he also imposed absolute authority on his subjects, which – in his opinion – was alloted to him from God himself. The puritans, among others, strongly objected to this – they even plotted a conspiracy to exterminate the king, but it was discovered, the conspirators arrested, put on trial and sentenced to death. This did not put an endto disputes about the monarch's, Parliament's nor the Puritans' positions in the nation. The effect was that, in 1611, the king was presented with the so-called *Apologies of the House of Commons*, which requested that he relinquish certain privileges associated with the king's position as England's highest authority. In 1614, the Parliament, in which the Puritans played a significant role, proposed to the king the so-called *Great Contract* (containing similar proposals to the *Apologies...*), yet the monarch not only rejected it, but also ordered the arrest of its initiators.

The Puritans found themselves in an even more difficult situation during the reign of Charles I (1625–1649), though in 1628 they did notice a significant success, which was parliament's passing of the *Petitions for Rights* (which included a request that the monarch observe certain ordinary rights and the protection of citizens). However, Charles I in fact did not intend to comply with the proposals it included (although he had committed himself to doing so), and as soon as he felt strong enough the first thing he did was to dissolve parliament (1629) and later he took firm steps against the opposition situated in the Puritan environment. They were removed from public offices and many were forced to seek refuge outside the country. Those who remained gathered their political strength in parliament, which due to the thirteen years' term (1640–1653), found its way into history and was named the "Long Parliament." In 1641, their supporters and sympathizers pushed through the *Great Remonstrance*, in which the unlawful practices of the king were condemned (including the imposition and collection of taxes without the consent of the House of Commons) and a request to limit royal power was put forward (through the staffing of royal advisor's offices with people approved of by parliament) together with an attempt to introduce economic freedom in industry and trade.

After a failed attempt to arrest parliamentary leaders, Charles I retreated to the north of the country and began to gather his forces there. This gave rise to several years of civil war (1642–1649), where on the one hand stood a less numerous, but well-trained royal army, consisting mainly of nobility, while on the other there was an army which consisted mainly of the burgesses. Divisions based on religion quickly appeared in the latter, that is, according to moderates (Presbyterians) and the more radical (Independents) led by Oliver Cromwell (1599–1658). His commanding and organizational skills displayed in the first and most difficult years of the civil war (among others at the Battle of Marston Hill) made the House of Commons adopt his project to open the New Model Army, and it entrusted him as its commander. The next important event in the history of the country was this army's defeating the royal army in several battles, and the arrest, bringing to trial, and sentencing to death of "the tyrant, traitor, murderer and enemy of the state" Charles I (the sentence was executed on January 30th, 1649), and the announcement of the creation of the English Republic (the Commonwealth). At first it was the internal feuds within the winning camp, then later the economic difficulties of the war devastated country and the need to deal with the aspirations of seceding Ireland and Scotland, and finally Cromwell's death that caused the country to return to the monarchical form of government (entrusting the crown to Charles II, the son of Charles I). But parliament still retained the stronger position. The social groups that played a significant role in these dramatic events were also well aware of their capacity to act effectively.

The social views of John Locke (1632–1704) are part of these historical realities. He was a philosopher and may be considered the spiritual father of liberalism – not only European, but also American (his thoughts inspired, among others, the authors of the Constitution of the United States of America). He came from a middle-class, rural family (his father was not a farmer, but a lawyer) who sympathized with Puritanism and the aspirations of parliament. He first directly encountered the strict variant of Puritanism during his studies at Christ Church College, Oxford (1652–1660), and later when he worked at the university as a lecturer (tutor). He was, however, discouraged by this activity to such an extent that he warmly welcomed the return of a parliamentary monarchy to England.

Lord Anthony Ashley's convictions (the later Lord Earl of Shaftesbury) in publically proclaiming civil liberties and religious tolerance, significantly affected John Lock's social views. Above all, however, these views were based on his own observations – made both in England and during his forced stay in the Netherlands (1683–1688), a country with a reputation for being one of the most tolerant in Europe. It was there that he wrote and published (in 1689) *A Letter Concerning Toleration.*[1]

The starting point for discussing its author's view of tolerance is the problem of the separation of the Church and the state. According to Locke, this separation could put an end to the manifold social conflicts and guarantee freedom of conscience. Freedom was brought by him "from heaven to earth," and placed into one group, along with the goods that are owned by a private person and citizen. These goods should be protected by law, and this law should have nothing to do with divine judgments or the salvation of souls. It is to come from the hands of earthly legislators, whose task is to establish, enforce, and punish those who violate it. Here there is not and cannot be any tolerance. On the other hand, it can and should be in the sphere of religious belief, or – which comes out to one and the same thing – the sphere of conscience, which leads a person to adopt a particular religion. Concerning this issue, Locke refers not only to God, who does not give anyone the right to impose his religion by force, but also to the nature of the human mind, which "cannot be enslaved by any external violence."

In any case, in reducing the role of the divine element in the sphere of religion and religiosity, Locke goes much further, because in his opinion, Man (he spells it with a capital letter), by his very nature is not affiliated with any church, and by his own will attends (or not) a certain religious community, which in his opinion cultivates true religion and true religiousness. Answering the question: what should the state's (secular institutions') attitude be towards different churches? – Locke's reply is clear-cut: neutral, that is, neither should

[1] Cf. J. Locke, *A Letter Concerning Toleration*, London 1812.

the state support a church, nor present obstacles for it to fulfill its social mission. However, it should also not tolerate such dogmas and religious or quasi-religious practices that come into conflict with morality and cause a threat to social order. According to him, such a threat, among others, was posed by atheists.

As he wrote in *Two Treatises of Government* in the years 1660–1661 (which appeared in print in 1667), Locke tried to show (as opposed to Sir Robert Filmer, the author of the work *Patriarch or a Defense of the King's Natural Power against the Unnatural Freedom of the People*, in which he defended monarchical absolutism) that every man is born free, that is, an individual can put into order their person and their property. He is free, however, only when he is not guided by some irrational impulses or desires, but by a reason that inclines him to ensure that "no one ought to harm another in his life, health, liberty, or possessions."[2] Locke sees the hand of the omnipotent and infinitely wise Creator in equipping humans with the special ability to reason. But how it is used depends on man himself. He uses it in a bad way when he tries to make other people his slaves, and when they oppose this, they enter into a state of war, a condition that essentially opens the door to many different types of crimes. To avoid this situation, using reason, a person should relinquish part of their freedom on behalf of public authorities, meaning entering into political or civic life.

It is such a society that determines it rights and safeguards their implementation. These rights primarily include the right to appoint the legislative, executive and federal authorities of the community. The first of these "is that, which has a right to direct how the force of the common-wealth shall be employed for preserving the community and the members of it;" the second is appointed for "the execution of the laws that are made, and remain in force;" while the third "contains the power of war and peace, leagues and alliances, and all the transactions, with all persons and communities without the common-wealth." The first of these – also called by Locke the *legislative* – ought to be in reality the highest authority, that is, all others must obey it, but because it originates from the people, it can also be revoked by the people if they consider that either it does not perform its tasks, or does not perform them with appropriate care. If the legislature's authority can be personally separated from the executive and federal (they can be exercised by different people), then the latter two should be in the hands of one person (the separation of their personnel might lead to "chaos and destruction"). Such a person should be, according to Locke, equipped with a so-called prerogative. This person is the monarch. In general

[2] Cf. J. Locke, *Two Treaties of Government*, New York 1963, p. 311 ff.

postulates, this philosopher is in favour of a parliamentary monarchy as the form of government which is best suited for England.

Neither Charles II of England (1660–1685) nor his brother James II (1685–1688) taking the throne after him wanted to agree to this form of government. The first tried to deal with the opposition by dissolving the old and appointing a new parliament (the so-called *Cavalier Parliament*), in which the supporters of an absolute monarchy had a distinct advantage. He issued a number of legal acts aimed both at the Catholic and Puritan religious communities.[3] The second brother too tried to deal with the opposition against the royalists coming from the Puritan circles (called *Tories*). *The Declaration of Religious Tolerance* published in 1687 by the parliament that favoured him, ensured among other things freedom of worship. This mobilized the opposition to the extent that in the years 1688–1689 they led the so-called "Glorious Revolution."

As a result, James II abdicated and William III of Orange (1689–1702) received the English throne. The latter had no intention, or perhaps just enough strength, to effectively oppose the aspirations of the English parliament and become the main authority in the country. These aspirations gained him legal sanction first by the presenting (in February 1689) of the *Declaration of Rights,* then the *Act of Tolerance* and the *Bill of Rights.* Nevertheless, they limited the scope of the royalty's power, including abolishing the right of the king to suspend the power of laws and requiring him to obtain parliamentary approval to impose and collect taxes, drafting men into the army, etc. It was mostly Protestants coming from the wealthy bourgeoisie and great landlords who benefited from these and subsequent legal acts. The successors of William III – his daughter Anna (1702–1714), George I (1714–1727) and George II (1727–1760) from the House of Hanover – also looked after their interests. As a nation, England established its political and economic spheres during a period of stability, whereas it entered the sphere of intellectual life in the period of the Enlightenment. The nation's intellectual notables are such philosophical giants as George Berkeley (1685–1753) and David Hume (1711–1776), as well as scientists and inventors such as William Herschel (1738–1822) and James Watt (1736–1819).

Among these notables were also thinkers who over time have made a significant contribution to European liberal thought. The philosopher and economist Adam Smith (1723–1790) is one of them. Already as a youth, in

---

[3] "The Act of Corporations of 1661 demanded swearing an oath according to the English formula by people possessing any office. *The Act of Uniformity* of 1662 was required for all priests of the Anglican Church. *The Conventicle Act* of 1664 forbade any public service of worship apart from those organized by the Church of England." H. Zins, *Historia Anglii* [The History of England], Wroclaw – Warsaw – Cracow 2001, p. 216.

his dissertation entitled *The Theory of Moral Sentiments* (1759), he revealed that he closely perceived man as a being living in relationship with nature and drawing from it – albeit usually unconsciously – everything that is necessary for him to live in a humane manner. The most important of his works was the *Inquiry into the Nature and Causes of the Wealth of Nations* published in 1776. In it, he reiterated his earlier formulated thesis, the idea that people strive for their own advantage, "are led by an invisible hand," and "often unwittingly and unconsciously" contribute not only to their own benefit, but also the good of society. In each case, the basis of this good should be work – in the past it was individual, but as time passes it increasingly becomes collective, until it reaches a point where the majority of the nation works for the common good.[4] In the past, the effectiveness of this work was due mainly to the professional competence of particular individuals. However, as time went by, the social division of labour and the conditions for trade and commerce began to play a greater role. The ultimate moment of these changes is the situation in which "society is actually becoming a trading community." For the existence and maintenance of this situation, however, a system of "perfect freedom" is needed, that is, one which, on the one hand allows for the development of the natural tendency for people to become rich, while on the other, becoming wealthy is not done at the expense of those who have a share in the manufactured goods, but at the expense of those who for various reasons do not have a significant impact on their distribution. In particular, this concerns the so-called "simple people," meaning all those who work as hired hands and live on the wages they receive from their employers.

These ideas were developed and disseminated by a group of thinkers creating the so-called classical school of political economy. Among them were David Ricardo (1772–1823) and Thomas Robert Malthus (1766–1834). The first, in his *Principles of Political Economy and Taxation* (1817) argued that while the value of goods is derived from the amount of labour necessary to produce them, yet their market price depends not only on their value, but also on many other factors – such as for example the agricultural producer's soil fertility, the industrialist's machinery equipment, and in both cases the demands of their markets.[5] In his conclusions and postulates, Ricardo far exceeded those of the realm of the economy and entered into social philosophy. On the basis of the latter, he formulated the thesis of the constant conflict of interests between employers and employees in industrial production, and its direct ties with conflicts between industrialists and landowners. This conflict is never

[4] A. Smith, *Inquiry into the Nature and Causes of the Wealth of Nations*, London 1776, p. 3.

[5] Cf. D. Ricardo, *The Principles of Political Economy and Taxation*, London 1821.

more evident than in terms of wages – an increase in wages always leads to a reduction in profits – but their reduction increases profits.

T. R. Malthus in his treatises entitled *An Essay on the Principle of Population* (1798) showed that over fertility occurring among the poor is one of the main causes of their misery.[6] In it, he formulated the general principle that an increase in industrial and agricultural production is always much slower than the accompanying population growth.[7] He calculated that the then-existing trends of development, after 75 years, would result in the number of consumers to be more than double the amount of the supply of food. In this situation, rational planning should involve not only the production of goods, but also procreation and population growth. Traditionally, this last ratio was significantly influenced by war, epidemics and various natural disasters (droughts, floods, earthquakes, etc.). Malthus did not put these factors into his demographic variables. Instead, he put emphasis on conscious sexual abstinence and the activities of the churches, which should foster activities conducted by the state in this area. Anyhow, he himself was a clergyman (a pastor of the Church of England).

For both thinkers, their sources of inspiration were not only Smith's, but also Jeremy Bentham's thoughts (1748–1832) – the author of many essays taking on legal, economic and philosophical issues. He made his debut in 1776 with *Fragments about the Government*, a work forming a polemic with the conservative views of William Blackstone concerning constitutional law. His adversary's error was not even that he relied on the fact that he drew from divine creationism, but that he would not allow changes to these beliefs. In Bentham's view, the value of law is social usefulness, and so it must be changed when it loses this trait. In 1789, he published his Introduction to the *Principles of Morals and Legislation*, a treatise in which the principle of utility was made the basis for regulating social life.[8] Its essence was to be the inherent drive in every human for the pursuit of pleasure and avoidance of pain. The desire to maximize pleasure is the main motive of human activity, but utility is – in the opinion of the author of the essay – that which distinguishes desirable from undesirable things. The principle of utility guides people not only in personal activities, but also collective activities, including the activities of nations in

---

[6] Cf. T. R. Malthus, *An Essay on the Principle of Population*, Cambridge 1992.

[7] "The warning note sounded by his work, in spite of his vaguely philanthropic intentions, had a remorselessly conservative significance. Your misery, he seemed to say to the working class, is your own fault. Your improvidence and lack of self-control has led you to multiply to the point of murderous mutual competition. You are wrong in blaming your masters, who share the ill-effects of your fault; for what is the poor-tax but the contribution paid by the rich to assist the improvidence of the poor, and to give them new incentive to the increase of population?" Cf. G. de Ruggiero, *The History of European Liberalism*, Boston 1959, p. 109 ff.

[8] Cf. J. Bentham, *An Introduction to the Principles of Morality and Legislation*, Oxford 1909.

carrying out trade with other nations, and they are mutually benefited by this. This ought to take into account public authorities, including the government, which has the legitimacy to act as long as it contributes to the relatively highest degree of the greatest happiness for the greatest number of members of the community.

Considering the different forms of government, Bentham spoke in favour of the so-called "representative democracy" ("acting by means of delegation"), and he was against any form of aristocratism. At the core of this democracy is both a belief in the individual person who, acting in his own interest, also works for the good of the community of which he is a member, as well as the belief in the collective wisdom of the community, which will not abuse its advantage over the individual. The task of a government is to regulate the relationships between individuals and collective actions so that they do not lead to discrepancies but rather the convergence of interests. This task is to be accomplished by influencing the wills and bodies of citizens through the appropriate use of a system of punishments and rewards. The list of the responsibilities of a government, which turns out to be not so much the "lord and master" as the "main provider," is obviously longer and is located in the central place of this great system of everyone providing each other with the reciprocal service of a well-organized society.[9] These views in pre-revolutionary France were already met with sympathetic interest. Revolutionary France gave its author honorary citizenship in 1792. In England, its supporters were, among others, James Mill and his son John Stuart Mill.[10]

2. Liberalism in the 19th and early 20th centuries

In the 19th century, Great Britain had rather good economic conditions, and science and art began to develop, but at the same time it was experiencing serious problems in its system of authority. At the summit was George III, a king with aspirations to play a much greater role than had been appointed

9 "Service comprises a principle category of Bentham's political thought. [...] All interpersonal relations are reduced to the all-encompassing system of services. A clergyman provides services to a faithful person, instructs him as to how to avoid eternal damnation; a wife provides her husband with services, satisfying his sexual desires; even a criminal, when he is captured and sentenced to punishment, provides services (though against his will) to society..." Z. Rau, *Liberalizm. Zarys myśli politycznej XIX i XX wieku* [Liberalism. An Outline of Political Thought in the XIX and XX Centuries], Warsaw 2000, p. 27.

10 James Mill cooperated with both Bentham (they even lived in the same house for several years), and Ricardo. He presented his views among others in *Commerce Defended* (1808) and in *Elements of Political Economy* (1829).

him by parliament. He tried to obtain greater power by appointing mediocre government positions to ministers that were obedient to him. Parliament itself was also not doing very well. Its main sins were not only the adoption of laws creating more losses than benefits, but also passively watching the actions of the royal ministers and the parliamentary factions supporting them (the so-called "friends of the king"). Severe clashes between supporters and opponents of the king occurred, however, only when the policy mistakes towards the North American colonies first led to war and then to their detachment from the metropolis.[11] The latter was represented by, among others, Charles James Fox – whose parliamentary speech eventually led to the resignation of Lord Norham's incompetent government in 1781. In the early 1780s, John Cartwright presented the draft reform of the English parliamentary system. The *Parliament Reform Association* that he founded called for expanding the right to vote, freedom of the press, and a further reduction of the royal prerogatives. These ideas were successfully opposed by the House of Lords. William Pitt the Younger, who was the prime minister from the years 1783 to 1801 and from 1804 to 1806 managed to achieve little to improve the functioning of the English parliamentary system. A draft electoral law reform prepared by him in 1785 (one of its components was to be the so-called elimination of the "rotten" electoral districts) did not obtain parliament's support. However, he first had to face such challenges as the revolution in France, and later Napoleonic expansion.

The United Kingdom emerged victorious after this confrontation with France. It was not only a military victory, but also political (among others, expressed by the expansion of colonial influence), and economic (cheap English goods found customers in the "French" surplus markets). This confrontation also had a significant impact on the political life in the country. Inspired by the liberal ideology of the French Revolution's motto, they admittedly met with a firm *votum separatum* – dissent from the conservative forces (Edmund Burke, author of *Reflections on the Revolution in France*, expressed these views) – but at the same time the favourable attention of those who called for changes in social relations. In the late 18th and early 19th centuries, Thomas Paine (1737–1809),

[11] "In 1765, the English Parliament passed two laws restricting the rights of the colonists in a hard way: The Quartering Act, authorizing the government to send an unlimited number of troops to the colonies and lodging them in private homes, and the Stamp Act, with collecting payments from stamps for all types of documents, newspapers, brochures and ads. Both these laws caused a huge uproar and led to riots, especially in Boston. [...] The Colonies adopted a proposal from Massachusetts calling for a nationwide Congress in Philadelphia in 1774, which passed the *Declaration of Independence* in 1776." Qtd. after H. Zins, *Historia Anglii* [The History of England], op. cit., p. 248.

author of the work *Human Rights* (he postulated in it the introduction of universal suffrage), exposed these views; and in the first half of the 19th century, a great and largely successful battle with the conservatives was fought.[12]

In the second half of the 19th century, England experienced a real economic boom. It was visible especially in large urban centres – such as London (the commercial and financial centre of the country), Liverpool (the main commercial port), and Manchester (the capital of the textile industry).[13] The development of industry and trade entailed the development of agriculture, which in the fight against foreign competition benefited both from a protectionist policy, as well as from modern technology. This economic prosperity primarily favoured the richest part of English society – a confirmation of this is witnessed, among other statistics, by the sharp increase in the number of large firms and business companies. (Henryk Zins states that in 1864 alone, "975 new companies was recorded in England with a total capital of 235 million pounds.") However, the middle-income social groups benefited from this too. It brought the least benefits to those employed in industry and agriculture. Nevertheless, even their wages and working conditions underwent improvement at this time. They had, moreover, their share in it – those affiliated with trade unions were so strong that employers had also to reckon with them.

The issue that continued to produce major social controversies in England at this time remained the electoral system. Its modification in 1832 gave only about 20% of the population of the country the right to vote, of which, additionally, only 10% were mercenary employees.[14] Perhaps due to this, they too were the main force in the struggle for universal suffrage for men. Radical liberals supported them in this in the second half of the nineteenth century, including John Stuart Mill (1806–1873), Herbert Spencer (1820–1903), and Thomas Hill Green (1836–1882), and in the first decades of the next century they included such people as Leonard Hobhouse (1861–1929).

---

[12] John Gray calculating the success of these forces points to the push through parliament in 1829 of the *Catholic Emancipation Act*, in 1832 the *Reform Act*, and the abolition of the *Corn Laws* in 1846. Cf. J. Gray, *Liberalizm* [Liberalism], Cracow 1994.

[13] "At the end of the fifties of the nineteenth century, England's share in the total global industrial factory production was approximately 50% and world industrial exports at 40%. [...] The export of British goods in the period from 1850 to 1859 exceeded by 44% the amount from the previous decade. In the two decades between 1850 and 1870, it increased from 71 million to 200 million pounds, while imports were at around 100 million to 300 million pounds." Qtd. after H. Zins, *Historia Anglii* [The History of England], op. cit., p. 287 ff.

[14] "In England, the property census was in force, which deputy candidates were subject to. It came out to 30 pounds of assets in the cities and 600 pounds in the countships. [...] In 1858, this passive electoral census was abolished, which was not, however, of great importance, because the vast majority of wealthy people were still being elected." Ibidem, p. 293.

J. S. Mill acquired his knowledge of liberal ideals and problems from his family home. His father – James Mill – was a highly regarded historian within liberal circles, an economist, philosopher and a journalist, supporting the reform of the English parliamentary system through use of his pen. He himself educated his son, selecting such readings for him which in his opinion would give him both a thorough and a useful knowledge – in his childhood these included, among others, the *Lives and Views of Famous Philosophers* by Diogenes Laertius, while later on in his youth it was the French Enlightenment philosophers (including Helvetius), and the English ones (including J. Bentham) that he read. The views of the latter seemed so important to J. S. Mill that, for their development and dissemination, in 1823 he founded the Society of Utilitarianism. For this purpose, he wrote a treatise entitled *Utilitarianism* (1861). In it he tried to annul the confusion associated with the principle of utility and explain what was going on and what utilitarians meant by their philosophy, through which he states:

"But to speak only of actions done from the motive of duty, and in direct obedience to principle: it is a misapprehension of the utilitarian mode of thought, to conceive it as implying that people should fix their minds upon so wide a generality as the world, or society at large. The great majority of good actions are intended, not for the benefit of the world, but for that of individuals, of which the good of the world is made up; and the thoughts of the most virtuous man need not on these occasions travel beyond the particular persons concerned, except so far as is necessary to assure himself that in benefiting them he is not violating the rights – that is, the legitimate and authorized expectations – of anyone else. The multiplication of happiness is, according to the utilitarian ethics, the object of virtue: the occasions on which any person (except one in a thousand) has it in his power to do this on an extended scale, in other words, to be a public benefactor, are but exceptional; and on these occasions alone is he called on to consider public utility; in every other case, private utility, the interest or happiness of some few persons."[15]

It follows that the utilitarian is – above all else – an individualist, meaning someone who most of all thinks of themselves and their loved ones, and achieves his own interests, and that there is nothing wrong with this as long as it is not "manifestly harmful to society." This is without a doubt one of the most important points joining utilitarianism and liberalism – in both cases, the individual person is found at the center; and we should add that this person is conscious both of his powers and his duties.[16]

---

[15] J. S. Mill, *Utilitarianism*, London 1879.

[16] J. S. Mill explains this on the basis of the relationship between utility and justice – "If it is a duty to do to each according to his deserts, returning good for good as well as repressing evil

He presented these broader powers and responsibilities in his treatises *On Liberty* (1859). According to the views he presented here, a basic human and civil liberty is the right to achieve one's "desires and instincts," while the primary responsibility is to not harm others. This arises from civic or social freedom, and the system of public authority. In any case, the justification for the existence of this public authority is for it to regulate the relationship between the individual and the collectivity in which the individual happens to live. The problem is that at different times and in different places people have different desires, social harms are differently conceived, and there are various methods of executing authority. As an example, J. S. Mill gives us among others the governments of former political tyrants. The subjects who agree to the tyrant's government do use their free will to some extent, but do not enjoy the usual freedom of citizens. This last fact in any case cannot be reduced to "selling oneself to slavery."[17]

There was an attempt to limit the power of tyrants "by obtaining a recognition of certain immunities, called political liberties or rights, which was to be regarded as a breach of duty in the ruler to infringe, and which if he did infringe, specific resistance, or general rebellion, was held to be justifiable"

---

by evil, it necessarily follows that we should treat all equally well (when no higher duty forbids) who have deserved equally well of us, and that society should treat all equally well who have deserved equally well of it [...]. This is the highest abstract standard of social and distributive justice; towards which all institutions, and the efforts of all virtuous citizens, should be made in the utmost possible degree to converge" (ibidem, p. 106 ff). It is worth noting that these and similar explanations many times appeared to be insufficient to dismiss criticism of the utilitarian conception of man. The criticism was made not only by the opponents of liberalism but also by some of its adherents such as e.g. John Gray who wrote: "According to a conventional view, no project could be more hopelessly misconceived than the enterprise of attempting a utilitarian derivation of fundamental rights. We are all familiar – too familiar, perhaps – with the arguments that support this conventional view, but let us review them anyway. We may begin by recalling that, whereas the defining value of utilitarianism – pleasure, happiness, or welfare – contains no mention of the dignity or autonomy of human beings, it is this value which utilitarianism in all its standard forms invokes as the criterion of right action. Worse, in so far as utilitarian policy must have as its goal the maximization of welfare conceived as an aggregate summed over the utilities of everyone affected, legal and political utilitarianism seems bound to have a collectivist bias, trading on the dangerous fiction of a social entity and ignoring the distinctness of separate selves with their several incommensurable claims." J. Gray, *Liberalism. Essays in Political Philosophy*, New York 1989, p. 120 ff.

[17] "His voluntary choice is evidence that what he so chooses is desirable [...] But by selling himself for a slave, he abdicates his liberty; he foregoes any future use of it, beyond that single act. He therefore defeats, in his own case, the very purpose which is the justification of allowing him to dispose of himself [...]. The principle of freedom cannot require that he should be free not to be free. It is not freedom, to be allowed to alienate his freedom." J. S. Mill, *On Liberty*, London 1851, p. 257.

and later by "the establishment of constitutional checks; by which the consent of the community, or of a body of some sort, supposed to represent its interests, was made a necessary condition to some of the more important acts of the governing power." With time, the last of these ways to limit the power of tyrants became "everywhere the main objective of lovers of freedom."[18]

In the treatises *Considerations on Representative Government* (1861), J. S. Mill presented his ideal of public authority. At its core is the assumption that "man, in order to protect himself from other people's malice, is only able to defend himself, by himself." It follows that the best system of authority is one in which "every citizen not only has a voice in performing this power, but is sometimes appointed to actually participate in the government, holding positions of local and general public authority."[19] J. S. Mill distinguished two variants of the exercise of such power by all citizens. The first is the democracy of equity ("it is the government of all the people by all of the people equally represented"), while the other is the majority democracy ("this is a government of the people by a simple majority of the people, which alone is represented exclusively"). A shortcoming of the first of these is the "tendency towards collective mediocrity" or also – what is one and the same thing – "the transfer of supreme power in the hands of people mentally standing much lower than the highest point of education which is obtained in this community."[20]

The weakness of the second system is making matters of interest easier for the majority at the expense of the minority communities. The ideal system of government should be somewhere between these two variants of democracy. In short, in the political system proposed by J. S. Mill, democracy begins "at the bottom," that is, at the level of the individual citizen. We should also add: such a citizen has such a degree of intelligence that allows him to understand not only his own needs but also the needs of others and the need to act in such a way so that he will not collide with the interests of others.[21] However, "at the top" is to be found the government, "in which all, not only the mere majority, was to be represented," and which – while maintaining the rights of

[18] Ibidem, p. 118 ff.

[19] From this assumption, he drew two "universal principles" – "The first is, that the rights and interests of every or any person are only secure from being disregarded when the person interested is himself able, and habitually disposed to stand up for them. The second is, that the general prosperity attains a greater height, and is more widely diffused, in proportion to the amount and variety of the personal energies enlisted in promoting it." J. S. Mill, *Considerations on Representative Government*, London 1861, p. 110 ff.

[20] An example of such a democracy was the United States in North America.

[21] In answering the question: how do we inculcate such intelligence in the folk people, such as "the worker who earns his keep by the work of his hands," Mill replies that the road leading to this is getting him involved in political discussions.

the majority to decide on the most important social issues – counted on the minority voice.

"The bit" which keeps the majority from attempting to pursue their particular interests ought to be the constitution, with its clearly defined rights concerning every person and citizen. In the treatises *On Liberties*, he primarily included the "liberty of conscience, in the most comprehensive sense; liberty of thought and feeling; absolute freedom of opinion and sentiment on all subjects, practical or speculative, scientific, moral, or theological." However, in the treatise *On Government*, he added to this list the following rules: equality before the law (without discrimination, among others such as gender and ethnicity), and representation, separation and controversy of authority, and the accountability of the government to the people, enforced by its constitutional representation, which is the parliament. The latter J. S. Mill proposes to make the most important of public authorities – not only more important than the government but also the king.[22] According to John Gray, Mill's views were not only conditioned by the times in which they came into being but they also transcend these conditions. They "meet needs which are enduring and widely felt. Mill's writings contain an argument for an open society which has not yet been decisively refuted, and of which every generation needs reminding: they are especially relevant to those sceptical of the claims of collectivist and totalitarian systems, who remain dissatisfied with any kind of purely defensive conservatism and seek a form of radicalism which is not afraid to contemplate the necessity of massive changes in current policies and institutions but which keeps a clear head about the dangers of all such large-scale social engineering."[23]

Close to J. S. Mill's liberalism are the views of Herbert Spencer, an advocate of naturalistic evolution and civil liberties. His understanding of evolution are presented among others in the article *Progress, its Right and Reason* – showing that evolution – which he called the "law of development" – is a widespread phenomenon, including both the animate and inanimate world, physical and mental as well as social development.[24] However, he first spoke about evolution in politics and the economy in the journal "The Economist," and later in

[22] In referring this situation to England at that time, he wrote: "By constitutional law, the crown can refuse its assent to any act of Parliament, and can appoint to office and maintain in it any minister, in opposition to the remonstrances of Parliament. But the constitutional morality of the country nullifies these powers, preventing them from being ever used; and, by requiring that the head of the administration should always be virtually appointed by the House of Commons, makes that body the real sovereign of the state." Ibidem.

[23] J. Gray, *Liberalism...*, op. cit., p. 1 ff.

[24] This law can be perceived both "In the geological and climactic evolution of the Earth, as in the evolution of society in all areas of life: political, religious and economic." Cf. H. Spencer, *Progress, its Laws and Causes*, in idem, *Essays, Scientific, Political and Speculative*, vol. 3, London 1891,

a variety of works – including, among others, in *First Principles*, 1862, or *Social Statistics*, 1851. In the first of these works he proved that these principles of rule should not only include evolution, but also "dissolution" (speaking about the occurrence of the reverse process of evolution), and the principle of homeostasis – in relation to society, it states that each "as a whole constantly strives to maintain a balance, consisting of adapting its population to the existing conditions of life."[25]

However, in the second of these, he added to this list the principle of "equal freedom" – this boils down to the fact that "everyone has the right to do whatever he wants, provided that it does not violate the same law for the other person." This means, on the one hand, leaving the individual person the largest possible freedom of action and, on the other, to reduce the role of the state to the necessary minimum.[26] In 1885, his dissertation was published, entitled: *The Man versus the State* – it is a defence of satisfying the needs of the individual and yet praises the state, which, in truth, does not help much in achieving this, but it also does not have to do so, and even should not do this.

Spencer's views, however, did not meet with such wide interest as J. S. Mill's. We could even say they were ignored in the middle of the nineteenth century and incorrectly understood and represented in the twentieth century.[27] Thomas Hill Green, professor of philosophy at the University of Oxford, enjoyed much greater appreciation at the time. His political activity was limited to participation in the electoral meetings of the Liberal Party. Yet he was a respected lecturer – his published lectures have significantly contributed to the popularization of "positive freedom," which, unlike the "negative" – which boiled down to the

---

p. 35 and others. He spoke about this most abundantly in his 10 volume work *The Synthetic Philosophy* (he completed the last volume in 1892).

[25] "This general principle" he wrote, "clearly appears in social activities. Supply and demand constantly adapt to each other in every industrial process [...]. Production and the distribution of products assumes a certain set of forces that cause specific types of special movements. The price of purchased products, however, is a measure of the strength of another set of powers, spent by the worker in other types of movements with different intensity." Cf. H. Spencer, *First Principles*, London 1945, p. 457 ff.

[26] Cf. H. Spencer, *Social Statics*, London 1902. According to Leszek Kasprzyk, in this work, Spencer does not calculate what the state can do, but what it should not do – this shows that the following should not be allowed: interfering in the economy, establishing a state church, helping the poor, directing education, having colonies and dealing with the issuing of money. Cf. L. Kasprzyk, *Spencer*, Warsaw 1967, p. 72 ff.

[27] "Reasons for twentieth-century neglect of Spencer's thought are many and complex. [...] Among the causes of Spencer's decline as a formative influence on thought, however, the prejudiced and ignorant treatment given his writing by moral philosophers of the late nineteenth and early twentieth centuries cannot be the least important. Like J. S. Mill, Spencer has been credited with a number of fallacies in moral theory..." J. Gray, *Liberalism...*, op. cit., p. 103 ff.

fact that a man has the right to "do as he pleases" – was not linked only with the duties of individuals living in a society, but also of the entitlements of the sovereign powers of public authority; one of these entitlements was to force a citizen to act in accordance with the existing laws in society.

Leonard Hobhouse, a professor at the University of Oxford (from 1897) and the University of London, propagated similar views. These views are presented among others in the work entitled *Liberalism* (1911).[28] In it, he not only made the distinction between negative freedom (from something) and positive freedom (to do something), but also pointed to their different forms. Within positive freedom, he included such things as: fiscal freedom (meaning limiting executive branch authorities in fiscal matters "imposed not only by fixed and written laws, but also through more direct and constant supervision"), personal liberty (freedom means both "in thought, speech, writing, printing and peaceful discussion" and "the right to religious worship in any form that does not cause injury to others or does not involve destroying public order"), social freedom (related to the "restrictions of individuals that result from the hierarchical organization of society," and are expressed among others in the "freedom to choose and practice a profession"), economic freedom (which means both "free enterprise" and the freedom of trade and services, as well as "expanding public inspection in industry and collective responsibility"), freedom of the family (including both "basing marriage on legal terms on the basis of a pure contract" and the "protection of the physical, mental and moral welfare of the children") and a few other freedoms.

[28] L. Hobhouse, *Liberalism*, London 1945, p. 21 ff.

Chapter 2

French liberalism

1. 18th century liberalism

French Liberalism came into being in the 18th century. However, its origins go back to the previous century. It was then that the feudal system of those powers and privileges for particular classes and smaller social groups was formed which served as an alternative proposition for people. Naturally, whilst they were limited, it cannot be claimed that virtually no one was free in the feudal system, since all social classes had their own liberties, which they did their best to protect. And any time they felt that their liberties were in any way threatened, they exhibited their full powers by staging rebellions. This was, among other factors, the starting point for the 1623–1648 wave of protests mounted by the poor peasantry. The immediate cause was the authorities' attempt to burden this part of the French society with extra fiscal services. In this, the peasantry were frequently supported by the lower and upper gentry as well as the lower clergy, i.e. those who perceived these additional services actually as a threat to the peasantry's ability to fulfil their seigniorial or ecclesiastical duties.

In 1648, the so-called Fronde of Parliament took place, in which the Parliament of Paris, dominated by the middle class and holding power over half of the country, rebelled against the policy of Cardinal Mazarin, who tried to limit Parliament's right to remonstrate, i.e. to express reservations about the King's ordinances. Later, between 1650 and 1653, that part of the aristocracy which did not go along with the absolute monarchy began to fight for its liberties. The so-called Fronde of the Princes was to some extent supported by the middle class and peasantry. Yet this proved to be the rebels' complete downfall, one of the major reasons being the fact that this internally diverse group only looked after its own interests. As a result, all the members of the Fronde lost out to the monarchical absolutism, which regained its power. Subsequently, Louis XIV, who ruled between 1661 and 1715, became an exponent of absolute power. His saying "I am the State" clearly depicts a situation in which the liberties of all the social classes concentrated on this central point of public life – which was represented by the monarch himself. Understandably, favourites of the king could benefit from this situation, but only as long as they remained among those who were favoured, and, which was crucially important in this particular case, as long as they managed to craftily flatter him.

Therefore, it should not come as a surprise that 18th century representatives of French liberalism considered speaking out against absolutism to be a matter of the utmost importance. One of them was Montesquieu, who criticized absolutism both in his *Persian Letters* (1721) and *The Spirit of the Laws* (1748). *Persian Letters*, written in the style of a traveller's book, features a Persian called Usbek who, while observing the everyday life of Paris, notes, among other things, that "in Paris, liberty and equality reign. Neither birth, virtue, nor even military service, however great these may be, distinguish a man from the crowd in which he is confounded [...]. They say the first person in Paris is he who hath the best horses in his chariot. A great man is he who sees the king, who speaks with ministers, who hath ancestors, debts and pensions. If he can, with all this, hide his idleness by an air of business, or a feigned attachment to his pleasures, he esteems himself the happiest of all mankind."[1] Naturally, all this is a manifestation of feudal freedom and a mockery of liberal freedom.

In *The Spirit of the Laws*, on the other hand, Montesquieu conducted a detailed analysis of monarchism. First of all, he distinguished it from despotism, and he could not think of any advantages for it. He described monarchy as "that in which a single person governs by fixed and established laws, a despotic government, one in which a single person directs everything by his own will and caprice." He depicts a monarch as "a man whose five senses constantly tell him that he is everything and that others are nothing," and who is "naturally lazy, ignorant, and voluptuous."[2] It would not be at all difficult to find in the above description any references to Louis XIV, especially when taking into account the final years of his reign. However, the task would be much harder in the case of his successors – the Regent of France, Louis Philippe, Duke of Orléans (1715–1723), and Louis XV (1723–1774). This is so because both of them were far from being able to identify themselves with their country. In his *History of France,* Jan Baszkiewicz described the former as "a trifler,"

[1] Montesquieu, *Listy perskie* [Persian Letters], Warsaw 1951, p. 142 ff.

[2] Cf. Montesquieu, *The Spirit of the Laws*, Cambridge 2006, p. 20.

and the latter as "a smart though lazy Sybarite keeping freedom in manners and morals."[3]

However, it is not these references to the two French monarchs that constitute the most interesting part of Montesquieu's characterization of monarchism but his attempt to compare its virtues and vices. He first considered the lack of the country's political stability as one of the disadvantages, since "if the whims and caprices of one person are what matters in a country, there can be nothing permanent, nor can there be any fundamental right." One of the advantages, according to him, was that the monarch functioned as a mediator between particular social classes and that he based his reign on the nobility, which acted as an intermediary between the monarch and the common people. He claimed that "the most natural, intermediate, and subordinate power is that of the nobility. This, in some measure, seems to be essential to a monarchy, whose fundamental maxim is: *without a monarch, there is no nobility*; *without nobility, there is no monarch*; meanwhile, there is simply a despot."

He immediately added that "it is not enough to have intermediate powers in a monarchy; there must also be a depository of the laws. This depository can only be political bodies, who promulgate new laws and revive the obsolete. The natural ignorance of the nobility, their indolence and contempt of civil government, require that there should be a body invested with the power of reviving laws from the dust and executing them, which would be otherwise be buried in oblivion."[4] Understandably, these "guardians" are courts of justice. On the basis of the above, it would be possible to produce a preliminary list of fundamental powers. It would open with the enlightened King supported by equally enlightened Ministers, to be followed by the Parliaments, which at that time performed a judicial function (there were twelve of them in 18th century France), as well as enlightened Parliamentarians.

In the second half of the 18th century, texts appeared whose authors evidently voiced their doubts as to whether the monarchs of France at that time were really enlightened. They even doubted that there was any possibility of enlightening them. One such author was Paul Henri T. d'Holbach, who dedicated his *Ethocracy or Government Founded on Morality* (1776) to "Louis XVI, the King of France and Navarre, to the Monarch who is just, humane, philanthropic; who is a friend of truth, virtue, austerity; who is an enemy of

---

[3] Cf. J. Baszkiewicz, *Historia Francji* [The History of France], Wroclaw – Warsaw – Cracow 2004, p. 270 ff. The same historian wrote that Louis XIV "undoubtedly had talent for both advertisement and self-advertisement," and that "he had enough intelligence to, for a long time, select for himself gifted ministers; yet he also made sure that they disliked each other, by which he managed to balance their influences." Ibidem, p. 249.

[4] Montesquieu, *The Spirit of the Laws*, op. cit., p. 45 ff.

flattery, depravity, tyranny; who is the restorer of order and good manners...," etc. However, even though this dedication was not meant to be a bitter joke about the monarch, it quickly became one. The above-mentioned French historian described Louis XVI as "a man with a weak personality and of mediocre intelligence," yet as the one who "raised his subjects' hopes after the long and bad reign of his grandfather."[5] The author of *Ethocracy* pointed to the lack of enlightenment not only among the rulers but among the subjects as well. In his Introduction addressed to the Reader (an enlightened one, of course) he wrote about "a mass of citizens who were ignorant and conceited or corrupt, who would consider even their most harmful habits as something sacred, their superstitions as fixed principles, their false beliefs as rigid rules, their pursuit of self-interest as the benefit to the entire nation, their injustice as undeniable rights."[6] If, at this point, the reader still had any doubts whether the author condemned feudal liberties (based on individual and foolish group egoism), subsequent parts of the work dispelled them completely since the writer strongly criticized the liberties of both the nobility and the clergy.[7] Such written works foreshadowed hard times for the so-called *ancient régime.*

It all started from summoning the Estates-General, i.e. representatives of the First Estate (the clergy), the Second Estate (the nobility) and the Third Estate (commoners: the middle class and the peasantry). Its first session took place on May 5th, 1789. From the very beginning, though, it turned out that the King and the Third Estate differed in their expectations. The former wanted to impose a general land tax, while the latter expected that at least this tax should be justly apportioned. At the same time they wanted the King to make a number of concessions (such as the permanent appointment of judges, guaranteeing the provinces their privileges as well as imposing a ban on the imprisonment of citizens without the court's permission). Understandably

[5] "He tried to fulfill these hopes by reforming the then political system. However, they failed to save the old regime, being too modest, inconsistent and, finally, soon being withdrawn to be replaced by new ones." J. Baszkiewicz, *Historia Francji* [The History of France], op. cit., p. 325.

[6] P. H. T. d'Holbach, *Etokracja czyli rząd oparty na moralności* [Ethocracy or Government Founded on Ethics], Warsaw 1979, p. 4 ff.

[7] In Chapter IV entitled *On Moral Rights for the Nobility,* he wrote: "to live a noble life means knowing nothing and doing nothing; going to war from time to time; it means idling persistently, intriguing, plotting at court; it means showing in public your glamorous clothing, teams of horses, servants and horses; it means plunging into financial ruin through gambling or for fallen women; it means drowning in debt and misleading your creditors; it means stealing and cheating" (p. 45). In Chapter VII entitled *On Moral Rights for the Clergy,* he judged monks and monastic life extremely harshly: "Despotism," he wrote, "provides the basis for a monastic government; this unjust and capricious reign can only shape slaves and hold power over those miserable ones who exhibit all the vices which enslave and debase the soul" (p. 81).

enough, the outbreak of a conflict was inevitable, whose results depended on the determination of both sides and on the cleverness of their leaders.

The disagreement arose when the participants differed over procedural issues, meaning whether voting should follow the principle: one man, one vote (*par tête*), or whether it should be conducted by the Estates. The first of these was far more beneficial for the Third Estate, which had the largest number of deputies (578) and, additionally, could count on votes cast by certain representatives of the other two Estates. After almost two months of dispute, Louis XVI gave in (on June 27th), which was followed by rapid changes. Already on July 7th, the Estates-General was transformed into the National Assembly (Constituent Assembly). On July 14th, the common people of Paris went out into the streets, seized weapons from the armoury at Les Invalides, and stormed the Bastille, the symbol of all the worst qualities of monarchical absolutism. On August 26th, 1789, the National Assembly passed the *Declaration of the Rights of Man and the Citizen*, which was meant to lay the foundations for the future constitution, which, to some degree, happened in the ratification of the Constitution from 1791. Also, the *Declaration* became one of the most notable features of the then French liberalism.

It has to be noted, however, that the *Declaration* is not a fully original document. The point is not that the text borrowed a lot from Montesquieu's works, but also that some of its articles followed the regulations of the American Act from 1776.[8] Even at first sight it becomes apparent how brief the text is, consisting of only seventeen short articles drawn up to solve the most essential issues concerning man and the citizen.[9] Perhaps this caused serious dispute and controversy, especially in the face of the different expectations of those social groups that demanded a change in the *ancien régime*, which became apparent during the first sessions of the Constituent Assembly. The so-called *Anglophiles* (with J.-J. Mounier as their leader) interpreted the *Declaration* mainly in the spirit of monarchism (no longer absolute but constitutional), while the so-called *Patriots* (including M. J. La Fayette and H. G. Mirabeau) leaned towards republicanism. Even more radical in their expectations and demands was "the street" (the common people), which was represented in the Assembly by J.-P. Marat and M. Robespierre, who did not approve of it at all. Therefore, when

[8] Cf. G. Jellinek, *Die Erklärung der Menschen- und Bürgerrechte*, 2nd ed., Leipzig 1904.

[9] It has to be remembered, though, that between May and August 1789, during the French National Assembly, more than 20 drafts of such declarations were submitted and discussed. Consequently, the resulting draft that was eventually approved by these representatives of the French nation was a compromise between its different fractions. All these drafts were collected and published by Christine Fauré. Cf. Ch. Fauré (ed.), *Les déclaration des droits de l'homme de 1789. Textes réunis et présentés par Christine Fauré*, Paris 1988.

the street took over power, it almost immediately (on April 24th, 1793) issued its own *Declaration of the Rights of Man and the Citizen.* Its preamble stated that the *Declaration* had been issued by *the common French people* and that *the people* were mentioned in all its thirty five articles. The last article stated that "when the government violates people's rights, insurrection is, for the people and each portion of the people, the most sacred of rights and the most indispensable of duties." This article clearly shows what *the people* and their parliamentary representatives lacked in the first *Declaration.* Briefly speaking, they lacked the true spirit of revolution, although the *Declaration* was the outcome of the Great French Revolution, and as such it became a permanent fixture in the changes the Revolution had brought about.

Naturally, the *Declaration* of 1789 has some other weaknesses and internal flaws. In his analysis of the *Declaration*, Guido de Ruggiero points to the fact that "it concerns more the rights of man rather than the rights of the citizen," and, what is worse, "places an abstract man above a concrete citizen." According to the *Declaration*, he says, natural laws precede the existence of the state as if law could exist without a state. In his view, it also contains "two elements of different sources and inspirations, juxtaposed with each other and mixed up, i.e. political freedom on the one hand, and, on the other hand, an individual's involvement in the creation of the State." He goes on to maintain that in the document "two democratic types of liberalism came face to face," the first of which "considered freedom as the possibility of doing everything that does not pose a threat to others," while the second type "assumes that power belongs to people. [...] However, both of them recognized freedom and equality as official and legally binding principles which aimed to sanction, and not to blur, the differences between individuals: people should be free in the sphere of their rights but equal in the eyes of the law." Additionally, the author states that "without a doubt, all that was in accordance with the spirit of modern individualism, which aims at developing human personality in the largest possible richness and variety. Equality before the law is a formal condition for the significant development of an individual's power in society."[10]

The then enlightened citizens must have been able to understand the statement "freedom is the power to do anything which does not harm another" as well as the explanation that follows it (in the same Article IV), which says that "the only limits to the exercise of each person's natural rights are those which ensure that the other members of the community enjoy those same rights," and, which is equally important, that "only legislation may set these limits," i.e. legal acts of the highest order. Presumably, the citizens must have

[10] G. de Ruggiero, *The History of European Liberalism*, Boston 1959, p. 68 ff.

interpreted in an unambiguous way the content of Article V, which says that "only actions harmful to the community may be made illegal. No one may be prevented from doing that which the law does not forbid, nor be forced to do that which the law does not command." It must have been the same with Article VIII, in which "only penalties which are strictly and clearly necessary may be established by law, and no one may be punished other than pursuant to a law established and enacted prior to the offence, and applied lawfully." However, more questionable might have seemed the issues raised in the first sentences of both articles, i.e. "only actions harmful to the community may be made illegal" (art. V), and "only penalties which are strictly and clearly necessary may be established by law" (art. VIII). The problem is that what is harmful to one community does not have to be so to another, or even to the very same community but existing in a different time period. The same can be said about penalties, which are indispensable for some communities, while for other communities they might remain only just possible or even redundant.

However, it is not the statements referring to freedom but those concerning equality that are the most ambiguous in the *Declaration*. Although in Article I the term equality immediately comes after the word freedom, its second sentence already raises some doubts by claiming that "general utility is the only permissible basis for social distinctions." It becomes obvious that the authors of this document did not interpret the equality of each individual as equality in every single respect (as this would expose common sense to ridicule) but as "equality of rights." Article VI clearly states that "legislation must be the same for all, whether it serves to protect or to punish," and that "all citizens, either in person or through their representatives, are entitled to contribute to its formation. As all citizens are equal in the eye of the law, positions of high rank, public office and employment are open to all on an equal basis according to ability and without any distinction other than that based on their personal merit or skill." However, all the rest remains just a matter of guessing. Therefore, on the basis of the above, one can only make educated guesses about whether if an individual is not socially useful (not necessarily of their own request), they cannot enjoy too high a social status among the social hierarchy, and they should not have overly great expectations from their society, either.

Does all of this mean that we should equate a beggar sitting in front of a church with a clergyman from that church, not to mention courtiers who live at taxpayers' expense? Another problem is how to understand the term socially useful. Does it mean that hard physical labourers are less socially useful (to themselves and to others) than those who are white-collar workers? The preamble's reference to the French people might imply that the former and the latter are valued equally. However, a careful examination of the articles that follow might raise more and more doubts in this respect. Would it be possible, for instance, for an uneducated peasant or a poorly educated artisan to hold "positions of high rank, public office and employment" in the same way as an educated person, experienced in public activity? I am convinced that for the authors of the *Declaration*, this idea would have been completely absurd. In fact, they did make attempts to explain that this was not the case.[11] Naturally, various "additions" and corrections were also made by the realities of political life prevailing both at the time of the Great French Revolution and long after it had come to an end.

2. 19th century liberalism

After the dramatic events that took place during the Jacobin Reign of Terror in France, nothing was the same any more. The slogan "liberty or death" written on the revolutionary banners, for many, including the revolutionary leaders like Robespierre, Saint-Just, Couthon, Brissot, Danton, and Hébert, meant death. It is estimated that as a result of this terror, approximately 35 thousand people were executed by guillotine. A significant number must be added to this death toll, hard to calculate precisely, of the victims of the wars fought subsequently over many foreign fronts (including those against the English, Austrians and Prussians) as well as internal fronts (against, among others, rebellious peasants, royalists and profiteers). Revolutionary France found it hard to establish the Committee of Public Safety; it was even more difficult to guarantee true salvation and safety for its citizens. These efforts finally met with some success, but the price was, among other things, the announcement of military conscription (by decree on August 23rd, 1793) of all men able to carry weapons.

Among these men was Napoleon Bonaparte, who first appeared on the political scene in 1791 as a Jacobin officer (and was quickly promoted from lieutenant to general); later, in 1799, he was one of the three, besides E. J. Sieyès and P. R. Ducos, who were dictators (also called *consuls*), and, finally, he became

[11] One of them was Antoine Nicolas de Condorcet, a member of the Constituent Assembly (he obtained his mandate from the Paris constituency), where he held the position of Secretary for some time. In his *Sketch for a Historical Picture of the Progress of the Human Mind,* Condorcet made it clear that all of this discussion was not about any equality but about attempting to avoid too great inequalities, but only in three spheres of human life, i.e. financial, professional and educational. At the same time, he believed not so much in the causative power of politicians and their political declarations but rather in natural processes which, among other things, "equalize people's properties in a natural way." Also, thanks to them, he says, people work more efficiently, and education is becoming more accessible to a larger part of the society." Cf. A. N. de Condorcet, *Szkic obrazu postępu ducha ludzkiego poprzez dzieje* [Sketch for a Historical Picture of the Progress of the Human Mind], Warsaw 1957, p. 224 ff.

an independent ruler and an "heir" to the whole of Revolutionary France. Formally, Bonaparte was appointed Emperor (on December 2nd, 1804) by Pope Pius VII, but in fact he crowned himself. A lot can be said about Napoleon and a lot has already been said thus far. Obviously, his supporters spoke of him favourably (calling him "a political genius"), while his opponents remained very critical of him (and called him, among other things, "a beast in human skin").[12] By no means, however, can anybody say that he was a liberal or that he sympathized with the liberals. Quite the opposite, he felt undisguised aversion toward them and even forced some of them to emigrate.[13] Therefore, later on, his final defeat in 1815 came to them as a great relief, although this meant that the powers of the Old Regime would once again go on the offensive. The offensive went down in history under the name the *Bourbon Restoration* (which meant an attempt to restore the situation from the pre-Great Revolutionary period), and it was again a very difficult time for liberals, since quite a lot of them lost not only their political but also professional positions. There was a particularly large number of such cases in education, which at that time was controlled by the Church.

The so-called July Revolution (from the 27th – 29th of July, 1830) put a stop to this attempt in order to restore the *ancien régime*. In fact, it was a street revolt provoked by a group of students and the journalists of "Le National" daily newspaper. One of its inspirers as well as its successors was Louis Adolphe Thiers (1797–1877). He described the social situation of France during the July events as follows: "Everybody kept saying that, with these open elections, with this genuine majority, with our government elected from among this majority, with the press that supports all this, one feels sufficiently free. No one demanded any more than that. And what did those most audacious head for? They headed for the realization that the Dynasty [the Bourbon dynasty – author's note] would never accept these conditions and that it would never accept this system either, and that it would be necessary to overcome this fundamental difficulty, i.e. to preserve the monarchy but to change the

---

12 For more information see J. Szacki, *Kontrrewolucyjne paradoksy. Wizje świata francuskich antagonistów Wielkiej Rewolucji 1789–1815* [Counterrevolutionary Paradoxes. The French Antagonists of the Great 1789–1815 Revolution and Their Visions of the World], Warsaw 1965.

13 One of those emigrants was a declared anti-Bonapartist Benjamin Constant (1767–1830). Zbigniew Rau describes him as a classical liberal of that time ("he became a leading figure in the pantheon of liberal theoreticians when he developed a modern concept of liberty"), but at the same time he emphasizes that "from a conceptual point of view, Constant's doctrine was far from being unambiguous," and that "Constant political thought cannot be reduced to one source of inspiration or, the more so, enclosed in only one trend of liberalism." Cf. Z. Rau, *Liberalizm. Zarys myśli politycznej XIX i XX wieku* [Liberalism. An Outline of Political Thought in the XIX and XX Centuries], Warsaw 2000, p. 33 ff.

dynasty. [...] If anyone wished matters to go beyond the monarchy, they did not express their wishes in public, in which they were right. France would not have taken this. The only thing one could afford to reiterate openly was that they were against any upheavals or revolutions and that they did not want that whole turmoil of 1793 to reoccur. They even wished that none of the theories of 1789 would reappear."[14]

Thiers knew perfectly well what he was talking about here, not only because he was an active participant of that strange revolution without a revolution, but also because he was sensitive about the social needs and expectations of the time. What is more, he possessed the ability to adapt to them and to craftily control them. Following the "Three Glorious Days" of 1830, France became a constitutional monarchy, with Louis Philippe (of the House of Orléans) as its sovereign and the so-called *Charter of 1830* as its Constitution. The white Bourbon Banner with three golden fleurs-de-lis was replaced by a tricolour one, and the King of France and Navarre's subjects now became French citizens. The monarch became the king of French people only, and to the traditional phrase "king by the grace of God" there was added the expression "and the will of the people." The *Charter* extended Parliament's rights, and reduced the minimum age electoral thresholds (down to 25 years in the case of active electoral rights and down to 30 years in the case of passive electoral rights). It also guaranteed freedom of the press and it appreciated the National Guard, the power which had played a considerable role in depriving Louis XVIII of his power.[15]

Naturally, the *Charter* was not revolutionary and the powers which had brought about the July Revolution did not expect it to be such. They expected, though, that the new government would remove from public offices those who had compromised themselves by attempting to restore "the old order," and replace them with those who, even if lacking titles of nobility, possessed sufficient qualifications to meet France and its citizens' necessities of life. To some extent, these expectations were fulfilled, which can be confirmed by, among other things, the amazing careers made by such liberals as Louis Adolphe Thiers and François Pierre Guillaume Guizot (1787–1874). Both of them came from middle-class families and both managed to secure the highest government positions in France.

Thiers was born in Marseille and studied law at the University of Aix-en-Provence. Next, he briefly ran his own legal practice in his home town. In 1821,

[14] L. A. Thiers, *La Monarchie de 1830*, Paris 1831, p. 10 ff.

[15] Nevertheless, it did not strengthen its position so that it could become a threat to its monarch. Louis Philippe enjoyed walking around in his guardsman uniform. The difference was that an ordinary guardsman had to devote his own financial resources for the necessary gear.

he left for Paris and began publishing his articles in the liberal "Constitutionnel" journal. Between 1823 and 1827, he wrote and published his *History of the French Revolution* in ten volumes and, in 1830, together with F. Mignet and J. Carrel, set up the aforementioned "Le National" daily newspaper. When Louis Philippe came to the throne, Thiers was appointed to the Council of State and promoted to Undersecretary of State at the Ministry of the Treasury. Later, he was the Minister of the Interior (1832–1835), the Minister of Commerce and Public Works (1833–1834), and finally the Prime Minister in 1836 and in 1840. At the time, he proved to be a man "with a strong hand" when, e.g. he put down the Royalist insurrection in Lyon and Paris. Also, his risky foreign policy which he carried out in North Africa almost led to a war between France and England. This was the direct cause of Thiers' dismissal from his government positions. Afterwards, for many years, he was an active member of the Parliamentary opposition, and in 1870 was re-elected Prime Minister. A year later, Thiers became President of the French Republic. However, France was now a distinctly different country from the one he had governed several dozen years earlier. There was a much smaller number of monarchists (even constitutional monarchists), while the republicans and social leftists (represented by, e.g. socialists) were growing in numbers. This became evident during the very dramatic events of the Paris Commune (March – May 1871). Thiers brutally suppressed this revolt, but this move did not meet with a lot of social approval, and his regime was criticized by the Right and the Left alike. As a result, in 1872, he submitted his resignation, and during the last five years of his life he was a member of the Parliamentary republican opposition.

Thiers presented his views on political governance in his study entitled *On the Monarchy of 1830.* He claims here that "the government takes a proper position when supported by the enemy's party and when its own party, or at least its vast majority, is slightly ahead of it. The government is lost, on the other hand, when it cannot resist its own friends or even break up with them so that it is not bound by any fraction."[16] What he meant here, of course, is that the government has to steer a middle course between various political powers. And so did Thiers, but for him there was not much room to manoeuvre – he stood between the liberal Right and the Left.

François P. G. Guizot was born in Nîmes into a family with strong legal traditions (his father was a barrister, executed by the Jacobins for his cooperation with the Girondists). Between 1799 and 1805, Guizot lived in exile in Geneva. Upon his return to France, he went to study law at Sorbonne University and became involved in anti-Napoleon youth associations as he advocated the restora-

[16] Ibidem, p. 87.

tion of the reign of the Bourbon dynasty. In 1812, Guizot was nominated chair of the Department of Modern History at his alma mater. In 1814, the year of Louis XVIII's reign, he returned to France and was appointed Secretary at the Ministry of the Interior. Napoleon's Hundred Days (March – May 1815) halted his office clerk's career for quite a long time. However, he remained politically active by supporting the so-called Party of the Doctrinaires, which advocated an English-style constitutional monarchy and fought against republican ideas. During the so-called White Terror (1820–1823), Guizot was removed from his university department and forbidden to continue any political activity. He focused more on writing, as a result of which he published a three-volume *History of Civilization in Europe* (1828) and a five-volume *History of Civilization in France* (1829–1832). He also wrote newspaper articles, mainly for the liberal "Le Globe." Guizot resumed his political activity at the beginning of 1830, when he was given a deputy's mandate. Then, in 1832, he first became Minister of Foreign Affairs and then Minister of Education, where he made himself known as a supporter of secular education for all citizens at the basic level. When, in 1840, Thiers' government fell, Guizot became Prime Minister and remained Head of the Government until the February Revolution of 1848, after which he withdrew from politics and turned to research work and to writing. Throughout this time, he wrote *The History of Parliamentarism in France* (1863) and *The History of France from the Earliest Times to the Year 1789* (1872–1876).

Guizot went down in history as the author of the slogan "enrich yourselves," though he was not a populist, so he did not have all the French people in mind here. He was a right-wing liberal, which meant that, according to him, mainly those who had enough zeal as well as sufficient financial resources could enrich themselves. As for social politics, on the other hand, here he referred to those who paid an income tax of 200 francs minimum per year.[17] From the point of view of Guizot's political philosophy, he brought the principle of social equality to the so-called "reasonable minimum." When asked what he meant by this minimum, his reply was that "all careers are available, there is free competition everywhere and everywhere authorities are linked with higher necessity."[18] He would say to those who accused him of having little in common

[17] This was quite a substantial tax and equaled a purchase of full electoral rights. The threshold began to be binding the moment the July Monarchy came into existence. In the 1740s, Nicolas de Dieu Soult's government advocated it (Guizot was Minister of Foreign Affairs there), while republicans and socialists preserved their critical attitude.

[18] In his reply to the question: "what does it have in common with his contemporary France?" he wrote: "It is true that the former privileges, exclusiveness and domination of aristocracy no longer exist; all careers are available for everyone; everyone is burdened with their duties, everyone is guaranteed the same personal liberties. It is justice but it is not social

with the equality which Revolutionary France had fought for, since "there is nothing more anti-social than equality; it is neither natural nor possible; each freedom is a privilege; each superiority is the beginning of aristocracy." His reply to those who tried to show him that it also had little to do with the freedom that came with the Revolution's banners (and bayonets), was that "after fifteen centuries of monarchy and sixty years of the Revolution, the Republic does not have appropriate conditions in France either for the government or for freedom. It offends, worries and ousts from the public affairs the social classes where the spirit of order and leadership prevails. It incites passions, ambitions and hopes in the masses which cannot be fulfilled by order or settled by freedom, and the masses strive for new revolutions." This means that everybody loses, including the revolutionaries. This, in turn, is a *votum separatum* towards revolutionism, but also towards republicanism and related to it democratism. Guizot put an equal sign between these and anarchism. Guido de Ruggiero did not call this period in history the July Monarchy but the Monarchy of the Bankers, about which he was quite right.[19]

Before the revolt of 1848, France already had ardent demo-liberals, also referred to as republicans on account of the political system they promoted. One of the more eminent republicans of this sort was Alexis Charles de Tocqueville (1805–1859). He came from a family with aristocratic and royalist traditions. His father, in recognition of his merits for the Monarchy during the Restoration, was nominated a peer (a member of the House of Lords in Parliament), while Alexis got the position of the judge-auditor at Versailles. As a young man, Tocqueville leaned towards the English-style constitutional monarchism (under the influence, among other things, of Guizot's lectures at Sorbonne). His journey to North America (1831–1832) turned out to be a critical moment in his life. He went there together with his friend Gustave de Beaumont in order to collect some information about the American prison system. The observations they made provided a basis for their analysis *On the Penitentiary System in the United States and its Application to France* (1833). However, the most significant effect of Tocqueville's stay in America was his *Democracy in*

equality; it is political freedom but not an exclusive rule of democracy. Varieties and inequalities of different types, like material or moral, natural or historical, exist and will always exist among us. In France, there are major, medium and minor owners, major, medium and minor manufacturers, grand surnames, old, new as well as unknown surnames which stand a chance of becoming grand if they have deserved this, but as long as they have proved not to be equal to those grand ones." F. Guizot, *Histoire parlamentaire de France*, qtd. after B. Sobolewska, M. Sobolewski (eds.), *Myśl polityczna XIX i XX w. Liberalizm* [Political Thought of 19th and 20th Century Liberalism], Warsaw 1978, p. 219.

[19] Cf. G. de Ruggiero, *The History of European Liberalism*, op. cit., p. 177.

America, whose two volumes were published in 1835 and 1840, respectively.[20] This work brought him recognition as a writer, and various honours. As a result, he was awarded the Legion of Honour and became a member of, first, the Academy of Moral and Political Sciences in 1838, and then, in 1841, of the French Academy. He was even given a deputy's mandate from the Department of La Manche in 1839. However, his republican views prevented him from accomplishing anything more.

His political position improved for a short while during the so-called Second Republic, i.e. between February 1848 and December 1851, especially during its initial period. This was possible owing to the fact that moderate republicans had united with moderate monarchists against radicals from the Left. Tocqueville was then appointed Minister of Foreign Affairs in 1849 and rapporteur of the Audit Committee on the Constitution. In December 1848, a presidential election was held in France, which was quite unexpectedly won by Louis Napoleon Bonaparte. On December 2nd, 1851, on the anniversary of Napoleon I's coronation, this "moron that can easily be manipulated" (Thiers' words) staged a *coup d'état.* The army, which remained loyal to him, secured strategic places in Paris. Meanwhile, the police arrested those deputies who had pledged allegiance to the new authorities (among them were Theirs and Tocqueville). After he was released from prison, the author of *Democracy in America* withdrew from political activity for good. At the end of his life, Tocqueville wrote another political treatise entitled *The Old Regime and the Revolution* (*L'ancien régime et révolution*), which provides an analysis of the attitudes of each particular social group of the French society of his time.

There is no doubt that Tocqueville wrote all his works with France and the French people in mind. Even when he wrote about America and the Americans, in fact he was thinking about his homeland. According to him, these two nations were similar in their love of freedom, and they differed in the way they understood the term freedom and in the way they put it into practice. In effect, Americans had a really democratic government, while in Europe, France included, one could only say that there were "democratic tendencies."[21] This is most visible in the electoral system, he said. American democracy is universal suffrage, and its general result is the blooming of the social virtues of the governed and... their disappearance in governing powers.[22] Tocqueville

[20] The great popularity of the book among its readers is particularly visible in the fact that by the outbreak of the 1848 revolt, there had been twelve editions.

[21] According to Zbigniew Rau, Tocqueville, in defending the American-style democracy, "did it in a way in which a typical conservative does." Cf. Z. Rau, *Liberalizm...* [Liberalism...], op. cit., p. 51 ff.

[22] "On my arrival in the United States," he wrote, "I was struck with surprise to discover the extent to which merit was common among those who were governed and how little there was

devoted most of his *Democracy in America* to the depiction of these virtues. From his description of this democracy there emerges a picture of America, and Americans, as a country of open possibilities and a people who want and who know how to take advantage of them.[23] Americans also feel less committed to theoretical studies, literature or art, for the sake of all that is practical.[24] In general, one might say that Tocqueville's book is in fact a "fresco" entitled "America and Americans."

He sharply contrasts America and Americans with the image of the then Europe, France and the French in particular. Hence, he claims that:

– In France, a guarantee for keeping the laws is sought for in the "administrative hierarchy;" in America, it is sought for in "elections."

– "In France, the constitution is immutable work, or supposed to be so." In England, "the constitution can therefore change constantly, or rather it does not exist." However, in America, the Constitution can therefore vary; but as long as it exists, it is the origin of all powers."

– Throughout all of Europe, political jurisdiction "Violates the conservative principle of the division of powers and that it constantly threatens the freedom and the lives of men. Political judgment in the United States makes only an indirect attack on the principle of the division of powers; it does not threaten the existence of citizens; it does not hang over all heads, as in Europe..."

Tocqueville, however, was not an uncritical apologist of American democracy. He pointed out not only to its advantages, but also to its various disadvantages and limitations, such as when so-called ordinary citizens elect as authorities people who are also ordinary people, if not mediocre ones.[25] For him, the greatest disadvantage of democracy is that it contributed to

among those who governed." A. de Tocqueville, *Democracy in America*, vol. I, Chicago 2000, p. 188.

[23] "In America, therefore, each finds easy ways, unknown elsewhere, to make his fortune or to increase it. Cupidity is always breathless there, and the human mind, distracted at every moment from pleasures of the imagination and works of the intellect, gets carried away only in pursuit of wealth. Not only does one see industrial and commercial classes in the United States, as in all other countries; but what has never been encountered – all men simultaneously occupied with industry and commerce." Ibidem, vol. II, p. 429.

[24] Chapter X of this volume is an attempt to answer the question: "Why Americans apply themselves to the practice of the sciences rather than to the theory?"

[25] "While the natural instincts of democracy," he wrote, "bring the people to keep distinguished men away from power, an instinct no less strong brings the latter to distance themselves from a political career." Then he went on to say that "in the United States, the people have no hatred for the elevated classes of society; but they feel little good will for them and carefully keep them out of power; they do not fear great talents, but they have little taste for them. In general, one remarks that everything that rises without their support obtains their favor only with difficulty." Ibidem, vol. I, p. 189.

the formation of a public authority that was overprotective. He described it as despotic because it takes upon itself securing people's needs and care for a citizen's fate. "It is absolute, detailed, regular, far-seeing, and mild. It would resemble paternal power if, like that, it had for its object to prepare men for manhood; but on the contrary, it seeks only to keep them fixed irrevocably in childhood; it likes citizens to enjoy themselves provided that they think only of enjoying themselves. It willingly works for their happiness; but it wants to be the unique agent and sole arbiter of that; it provides for their security, foresees and secures their needs, facilitates their pleasures, conducts their principal affairs, directs their industry, regulates their estates, divides their inheritance [...]. So it is that every day it renders the employment of free will less useful and more rare."[26] Thus, Tocqueville did not advocate transferring American values to Europe, not only because they contain the disadvantages mentioned in the quotation above, but also because that European communities have different traditions, customs, expectations and a wide range of other dissimilarities, which to casual observers might seem trivial while remaining fundamental for the communities that cultivate them.[27]

Alongside these two mainstream types of secular liberalism of the then France, i.e. aristocratic and democratic, there arose yet another type, which was religious in character. It brought together secular Catholics and clergymen who wanted to actively participate in the process of solving the social problems in their own country and to keep up with the political achievements of the Great French Revolution generation. At the time of the Restoration, they presented a threat to all those powers which tried to distance themselves from the revolutionary heritage. Their leaders were first centred around the "Mémorial" magazine, which began to be published in 1824, and then, after its liquidation in 1829, about the "L'Avenir" magazine. Among its most prominent figures was Hugues-Félicité-Robert de Lamennais (1782–1854).

Lamennais worked to protect freedom, just as other liberals did. However, unlike numerous secular liberals, he publicly defended God. He founded his own "L'Avenir" magazine which he subtitled "God and Liberty," where he claimed that "God and liberty have been the two great accomplishments of

[26] Ibidem, vol. II, p. 663.

[27] For example, the difference between the French and American press is visible at first sight – "In France, commercial advertisements take up only a very restricted space and even news items are not very numerous; the vital part of a newspaper is the one where political discussions are found. In America three-quarters of the immense newspaper that is placed before your eyes is filled with advertisements, the rest is most often occupied by political news or simple anecdotes; only from time to time does one perceive in an overlooked corner one of the burning discussions that are the daily fodder of readers among us." Ibidem, vol. I, p. 176.

Catholicism."[28] For him, the major problem that post-revolutionary France and French people were faced with was that these accomplishments were separated from each other. He put the blame not only on secular, but also on church circles, including the hierarchy of the Church itself. It did not take long for this to cause a reaction on the part of the Church hierarchy. Already at the beginning of 1831, the French Episcopate forbade the faithful to read his magazine. When, in reply to this move, its journalists appealed to Rome, instead of the anticipated support they were met with condemnation in the form of George XVI's Encyclical. This document, entitled *Mirari vos*, calls the ideas presented in "L'Avenir" "shameless" and states that their belief that "each individual should be guaranteed freedom of conscience" is simply absurd.

At first, Lamennais and a group of his closest co-workers from his magazine bowed to the Church's pressure and issued a public statement that "we are unable to continue our work without standing in contradiction to the publicly expressed will of the One whom the Lord granted power over the Church." Nevertheless, the more thought some of them gave to this situation, the more they started to openly defend their views. Lamennais was among them. He first wrote and published *Hymn to Poland* (inspired, among other things, by the November Uprising), followed by *Words by a Believer*. The latter was not only an open renouncement of their allegiance to the Church, but also a firm *votum separatum* to the status quo of Europe at that time. Predictably, this time, Rome's reaction was immediate. In June of that same year, another Encyclical was released entitled *Singulari nos*, which reads as follows: "this book contains proposals that are false, defamatory, audacious and such that lead to anarchy, which are contrary to the Word of God and therefore godless, disgraceful, improper, already condemned by the Church in its verdicts against Wycliffists, Hussites and other heretics."[29]

It must be admitted that, though relatively short, *Words by a Believer* makes a considerable impression on the reader. The author places himself on the Left, still liberal but already radical, which means that he demanded revolutionary social changes. He begins like a typical Christian, i.e. from calling on the name "of the Father, and of the Son, and of the Holy Spirit," and finishes like a new prophet of a religion in which no visible Church is required because he can hear God's voice in his own soul which he spreads to all the oppressed peoples

[28] "These are his two great necessities, necessities which are inseparable because every place where true faith in God is, liberty is loved; every place where liberty is, God is loved." "L'Avenir" from 2nd of January, 1831. Qtd. after A. Sikora, *Lamennais czyli dramat konsekwencji* [Lamennais or the Drama of the Consequences], *Wstęp* [Introduction], in H.-F.-R. de Lamennais, *Wybór pism* [Select Writings], Warsaw 1970, p. 54.

[29] Qtd. after ibidem, p. 76.

of the world.[30] These two extreme points are joined by a motif of Liberty (which he spells with a capital letter) – the people's Liberty and Liberty for the people. According to *Words of a Believer*, this Liberty is God's gift ("Christ brought Liberty down to Earth"); it is even the most precious of God's gifts because without it, no people can achieve happiness. It is also like "bread which peoples ought to acquire by the sweat of their brows." Hence, peoples make attempts to get bread but everything they manage to get is later taken away from them by secular and religious tyrants, like e.g. monarchs, "Christ's priests" as well as secular intelligentsia (frequently referred to as "hypocrites," who want to handle their own matters at the expense of their people). The book precludes the possibility of the oppressors' fraternizing with the oppressed. Lamennais calls the former "the children of Satan" and presents them only in a bad light. He claims that the worst are those who "plead the name of liberty" ("they combine falsehood with tyranny and injustice with desecration"). Lamennais perceives and depicts the social reality of his time as a world upside down, i.e. the one in which "the righteous beg for bread, the highest honours are bestowed upon villains, who possess untold riches, wicked judges pronounce unjust sentences on the innocent, idlers have an abundance of everything while workers do not have enough bread to make a living, clothing to cover their naked bodies, a roof over their heads, a bundle of straw to sleep on," etc.

According to him, only a revolution could change all this. Therefore, Lamennais called upon the oppressed peoples to stage a revolution by saying "liberate [...] your work, liberate your hands, and poverty will only become an exception, sent by God to people in order to remind them about the frailty of human nature and for them to remember that they owe each other help and love." At the same time, he warned them: "do not let yourselves be deceived by idle words. This and that will attempt to convince you that you are entirely free [...]. Liberty is not a placard which is put up to read on street corners. It is mighty power which we can feel in ourselves, a caring genius of hearth and home, a guarantee of social rights, with the right to freedom as the very first right."[31]

---

[30] "[...] Everything that has so far been hidden from me," he wrote, "has been revealed in front of my eyes, which before could not be stopped by the material layer of my being. Liberated from earthly ties, I moved from one world to another, and my soul, carried by the waves of harmony, was falling into slumber amongst the heavenly stream, in indescribable ecstasy. And then I beheld Jesus Christ at the right hand of the Father, and Jesus Christ was radiating with everlasting glory." H.-F.-R. de Lamennais, *Słowa wierzącego* [Words of a Believer], in: idem, *Wybór pism* [Select Writings], op. cit., p. 206.

[31] Ibidem, p. 161.

3. Liberalism of the Third Republic of France

Voices calling for a revolution in France finally began to be heard during the Paris Commune. During the dramatic months of February – May 1871, the Committee of Public Safety was formed anew. It soon turned out, however, that it was unable to save the entire society or even its most radical part from both external and internal threats. France lost the war against Prussia, with its capitulation signed on May 10th, 1871, under the Treaty of Frankfurt. The last group of the Commune members was slaughtered by general Galliffet on May 28th of at the Père-Lachaise Cemetery. After unsuccessful attempts to restore a monarchy (Count Chambord, a descendant of the Orleans branch of the House of Bourbon, insisted that his power came solely from God), the 75-year-old liberal Thiers came to power once again. Nonetheless, both the local and supplementary elections of 1872–1875 showed that the French nation had awaited not a liberal right-wing politician but a liberal leftist – at any rate, the one who would understand the republican ideas and who would be able to implement them in future internal politics. France one again became a republic after the so-called Constitutional Laws were accepted in February and July, 1875. France came to be called the Third Republic in order to clearly distinguish it from the extremes of the first two republics. While it had neither a monarch nor the House of Lords, it still had a president who possessed powers similar in certain aspects to those of a king, as well as the Senate whose members could perceive themselves as the nation's representatives standing much higher in hierarchy than members of the Chamber of Deputies.[32] Despite considerable criticism, the Third Republic lasted until 1940.

The Republic was criticized both by the Right and the Left, including left-wing liberalists, one of the most prominent of whom was Émile Faguet (1847–1916), the author of numerous works on liberalism, such as *Liberalism* (1902), *Anticlericalism* (1906), *Pacifism* (1908) and *The Cult of Incompetence* (1911). In 1890, he became a professor at Sorbonne and, in 1900, a member of the French Academy. In his books and numerous newspaper articles, which he published mainly in the liberal "Journal des Débats," Faguet engaged in polemics against his political opponents as well as different widespread convictions

[32] "The Senate was supposed to be the mainstay of conservatism [...]. A high age census (40 years of age), a gradual renewal of the Senate (1/3 every 3 years): all this was meant to foster the role of the Senate as a stabilizing factor, a brake on change. The Senate possesses the same legislative rights as the House, and additionally, it has the rights of the State Tribunal to judge the crimes of the President and Ministers as well as the gravest of political crimes." J. Baszkiewicz, *Historia Francji* [The History of France], op. cit., p. 489.

such as the one according to which an individual and a citizen is entitled to receive something from society only because he is a man and a citizen. He agreed that by his very nature a man is a member of society and that living in society makes him more human (today this is called socialization), yet at the same time he stressed the fact that an individual has no rights (i.e. powers) until "he renders some service or signs his first commitment."[33] In other words, if one expects to receive something from society, they have to give something in return or, at least, commit themselves to sacrificing something for the sake of the society, like their work, time, talents, etc.

Faguet blamed philosophers and politicians for popularizing among the citizens different demanding attitudes, including those who had drawn up the *Declarations of the Rights of Man and the Citizen* in 1789 and 1793 respectively. In his view, both of these documents are a kind of statement of faith – faith in man and the citizen who wants to and who knows how to get along with other people and, above all, who aims to "liberate himself from the state of despotism and to fight for as great a number of personal freedoms as possible." The problem is, however, that this faith, just like any other type of faith, is "complex," contradictory, one which tries to mix "water and fire."[34] These defects are particularly visible in the Jacobins' *Declaration*. Obviously, this is so because its authors had gone further than their predecessors from 1789, which means that they had upgraded not only liberty but also equality to the status of principle. In this way, however, this otherwise noble quest for equality was brought to the level of the absurd. In fact, people are not equal either by their nature (by birth) or in light of their rights.[35] Faguet discusses this problem thoroughly in *The Cult of Incompetence*, where the term cult means nothing but the principle of equality applied in full. He considered this principle to be contradictory to the obvious facts and to be socially dangerous since, as he claims, it contributes to the people's or Parliament's complete seizure of power.[36]

---

[33] Cf. É. Faguet, *Liberalizm* [Liberalism], Lvov s.a., p. 33 ff.

[34] "To place in the very same enunciation the rights of the people and the rights of man, e.g. the omnipotence of the people and the liberty of an individual, without any reservations, is like mixing water and fire in pious hope that they will coexist somehow." Ibidem, p. 38.

[35] "If you assume that liberty is a right of man, and that all people are equal by birth, destroy the community, which by itself had destroyed this natural law in which inequality reigns; do not content yourselves with equality by law, which, by itself, is barely anything and which, without real equality, is just a shallow joke. Instead, introduce essential equality, nature permitting, beginning with equality of the distribution of wealth." Ibidem, p. 45.

[36] He claims that there are attempts to oppose these aspirations by the introduction of the separation of powers. However, in countries in which voters "have neither a sense of liberty nor a sense of the rights of man, this omnipotent power, which people attempted to avoid, produces a new omnipotent power – the omnipotence of Parliament. They both stimulate

In his evaluation of the social situation of the Third Republic of France, Faguet points to two other threats. One of them is thoughtless egoism and something which is directly related to it, i.e. partisanship. He described the contemporary average Frenchman as "a passionate partisan who desires nothing more than to be successful in his own business, and for his party to triumph and to crush the opposing parties." The other threat is religious piety and the clericalism which is related to it. He claims that the average Frenchman firmly believes in the fact that his fate is not in his own hands but in the hands of Providence, in which clergymen, so numerous in this country, confirm him. In this case, the conclusions become obvious – the Frenchman ("who has been educated for over three hundred years by Catholics and Protestants alike") finds it difficult to be "an ardent liberal," while "the post-1789 France is one of the least free and liberal countries in the world."

In many respects, France is supposed to be "exactly the opposite of the American ideal and the American practice." It is there that true civil liberty is present, while in France "it is mainly pornographic publications that enjoy freedom of thought, speech and the press," and "only clergymen enjoy freedom of association," etc. Faguet maintains that the solution to these problems should, in the first place, be the establishment of a strong government. Each citizen is in need of a strong government: "freethinkers need one against monks, Protestant ministers and monks need one against Catholics, Catholics, in turn, need one against Jews and Protestants," etc. Faguet expects such a government to, among other things, formally and legally separate the Church from the state or, which is the same thing, to grant the Church "features similar to those of a private railway company." He is strongly convinced that these views he has are not meant to propagate any belligerent anticlericalism but rather modern (i.e. republican) liberalism.[37]

each other towards tyranny and push each other towards the extremes." Cf. É. Faguet, *Kult niekompetencji* [The Cult of Incompetence], Lvov – Warsaw 1922, p. 306 ff.

[37] "Following liberal principles," he added, "the Church is a free association of citizens who gather together and unite in order to pray to God, to talk about spiritual matters, to encourage each other to doing good deeds, to helping the poor. It possesses, if it so wishes, its own organization, hierarchy, discipline as well as budget and wealth. As for meetings and observing religious rituals, the Church is responsible to the municipal or rural police. When it comes to its wealth, it pays taxes at the same amount as all the others do." É. Faguet, *Liberalizm* [Liberalism], op. cit., p. 164.

Chapter 3

German liberalism

1. Precursors

In all cases, the ideas of the Enlightenment period provided the ideological background for liberalism. The problem with German countries is that these ideas became established only with considerable difficulty and were almost exclusively "imported" from France or England. A textbook example may be the court of the King of Prussia – Frederick II (1740–1786), otherwise known as the Great. Actually, it was he who considered himself "great," because – diligently following the suggestions contained in Montesquieu's *The Spirit of the Laws* – he abolished various forms of torture, universally employed in other European countries as a means of obtaining testimony from the accused, and put into effect the rule of equality (mainly in tax regulations). He also spoke only in French and was admired by the celebrities of the German culture (for example, Goethe) and other countries (including France).

However, even when one accepts a very broad definition of who a precursor might be, it seems seriously doubtful, if not even amusing, to consider this rather despotic king as the spiritual father of German liberalism. It is definitely easier to see such a figure in the Austrian Emperor Joseph II, whose understanding of the rule of equality was so literal that he wore a common soldier's uniform and, more importantly, abolished the serfdom of the peasants, issued an edict on tolerance (which in fact led to religious equality), liquidated all contemplative orders and began the process of "retraining" priests into civil servants.[1]

[1] In his characterization of these policies – generally known as "Josephinism" – a historian of the Catholic Church, Fr. Marian Banaszak, writes that "with his psychic predispositions

Leopold II, his successor, attempted to abandon Joseph's policy, but his rule was so short lived (1790–1792) that he did not manage to return to the old order. During the hegemony of Napoleon's France, in Europe, Joseph's policy was continued in the German countries and the changes proved so deep that even during the Restoration the results of going back to the pre-revolutionary order were barely discernible. It was indeed possible to attempt to free the Church from "the police surveillance of the state" (as Fr. M. Banaszak calls it in his *Historia Kościoła katolickiego* [The History of the Catholic Church]) by incorporating into traditional Christian values those which were part of liberal ideology. One of the people who took up this task was Franz Josef Buss, professor of law at the University of Freiburg.[2]

Among secular thinkers, some elements of liberal ideology appear as early as at the beginning of the 18th century – such as in the works of Christian Thomasius (1655–1728), a lawyer and advocate of natural law (as defined by Hugo Grotius), who propagated leaving a fair amount of freedom to the rational being. Some features of liberal ideology can also be found in the philosophical works of Immanuel Kant (1724–1804). Answering the question posed in the title of his programmatic essay "What is Enlightenment?" the philosopher writes that it is "man's emergence from his self-imposed nonage" and the act of entering the path of enlightenment, which "requires nothing but *freedom* – and the most innocent of all that may be called 'freedom': the freedom to make public use of one's reason in all matters."[3] Elements of liberalism appear also in Kant's Idea for a Universal History from a Cosmopolitan Point

(solitary, strict, determined, lacking a sense of humour, meticulous) the emperor was ruthless when introducing his reforms. As he did not understand the meaning of monastic life, he did away with contemplative orders, instructed others to pursue useful activities, such as nursing, education and science. [...] The priories were converted into warehouses, granaries and workshops, while the properties were given to the Religious Fund, which was used for financing parishes, and establishing schools and hospitals. [...] the parish priest was to be a kind of civil servant and educational activist; during the masses he was to read and explain the emperor's decrees, popularize farming and sanitarian knowledge, and fight prejudice." Fr. M. Banaszak, *Historia Kościoła katolickiego* [The History of the Catholic Church], vol. 3, Warsaw 1991, p. 17.

[2] "He tried to reconcile Catholic conservatism with liberalism, he developed Catholic corporatism and was the first to draw attention to the fact that the main objective of a Catholic, apart from fighting for Church liberties, is solving social problems." Ibidem, p. 84.

[3] But in 1784 he answered negatively to the question: "Do we presently live in an enlightened age?" He explained that "it is still far from true that men are already capable of using their own reason in religious matters confidently and correctly without external guidance." In Prussia, where he lived and for so many years was Frederick II's subject, this period was called "the century of Frederick" – "A prince [who] ought not to deem it beneath his dignity to state that he considers it his duty not to dictate anything to his subjects in religious matters, but to leave them complete freedom." I. Kant, "Co to jest Oświecenie?" [Was ist Aufklärung?], in T. Kroński, *Kant*, Warsaw 1966, p. 164 ff.

of View. He notes here that "the greatest problem for the human race, to the solution of which Nature drives man, is the achievement of a universal civic society which administers law among men. The highest purpose of Nature, which is the development of all the capacities which can be achieved by mankind, is attainable only in society, and more specifically in the society with the greatest freedom. Such a society is one in which there is mutual opposition among the members, together with the most exact definition of freedom and fixing of its limits so that it may be consistent with the freedom of others."[4]

Another distinguished German philosopher, Georg Wilhelm Friedrich Hegel (1770–1831) often makes anti-liberal comments, emphasizing the leading role not of the enlightened individual, but of the state. In his *Elements of the Philosophy of Right* he writes that "[w]ere the state to be considered as exchangeable with the civic society, and were its decisive features to be regarded as the security and protection of property and personal freedom, the interest of the individual as such would be the ultimate purpose of the social union."[5] He perceived such an approach as revealing an error of the subjective spirit or – which was the same to him – particularism. The expression of the objective spirit, i.e. Hegel's universalism (the realization of the Absolute Mind) is, according to him, not the individual, but the state, as "the individual himself possesses objectivity, truth, and ethical life insofar as he is a member of the state." However, as his discussion develops, there appears some leeway for liberalism. It is certainly not too prominent, because it justifies only that liberalism which opposes rulers' despotism and opts for constitutional monarchy.

In contrast, for Hegel the perfect example of such a state was not Prussia but Napoleon's France. The Prussian authorities somehow accepted this fact and appointed him the head of the philosophy department at Berlin University. He held this post until his death, acquiring in liberal circles the name of the "Prussian national philosopher" (which meant: conservative and legalist). Not until carrying out a close reading of his works can one find statements which correspond to liberal ideology, such as those which appear in his *Propedeutics of Philosophy*. He notes that "the human being is free. This is the basic attribute of his nature" and "the human being – because of external circumstances of fate and all he is in himself – must act in such a way that he creates his own fate and that the form of its outer existence is taken away from it."[6]

---

4 Ibidem, p. 174 ff.

5 G.W.F. Hegel, *Philosophy of Right*, Kitchener 2001, p. 195. Zbigniew Kuderowicz contends that Hegel's attitude towards liberalism "was always full of doubt." Cf. Z. Kuderowicz, *Hegel i jego uczniowie* [Hegel and His Disciples], Warsaw 1984, p. 39 ff.

6 G.W.F. Hegel, "Philosophische Propädeutik," in idem, *Sämtliche Werke. Jubiläumsausgabe in zwanzig Bänden*, vol. 3, ed. H. Glockner, Stuttgart 1927–1940, p. 246 ff.

2. Liberalism in the first half of the 19th century

After the end of the Napoleonic wars, no European country had good enough conditions for the popularization of liberal ideology. Obviously, the same situation existed in Germany (or, more precisely, German-speaking) countries. During and after the Congress of Vienna (1814–1815), the Austrian minister Klemens Lothar Wenzel von Metternich advocated an approach to liberalism which could be summed up in three words: "forbid, prohibit, close" (e.g. liberal periodicals). Conservative Europe, however, did not repulse Napoleon Bonaparte, who was one of the contenders to control everyone and everything, and it paid such a high price for the Napoleonic wars, only to fall under the rule of another aspirant. In other words, every single country had its own interests and was reluctant to sacrifice them in the name of an anti-liberal crusade. This became manifest already at the Congress of Vienna, where Tsar Alexander I and the King of Prussia Frederick William III refused to punish Saxony for remaining by Napoleon's side until the very end. The signatories of the Holy Alliance were actually aware that a significant part of their society supported liberal ideas and they had to be offered if not a constitution then at least, as in France, a charter which would resemble it. In the years 1814–1848, similar charters appeared in the southern German countries, for example the Kingdom of Bavaria and the Kingdom of Württemberg. In the countries where either the rulers were not too willing to make such fundamental concessions to liberalism or there was not enough pressure to bring them about, there still remained a possibility of popularizing liberalism through the universities.

In many cases, this opportunity was quite frequently taken. In his discussion on German liberalism, Guido de Ruggiero draws attention to the fact that to a large extent it found its representatives among university professors such as Carl Wenzeslaus Rotteck (1775–1840), Friedrich Gagern (1794–1848), Jacob Ludwig Karl Grimm (1785–1863) and Georg Gottfried Gervinus (1805–1871).[7]

[7] "The first struggles of university Liberalism were conducted within the schools and by academic weapons. Only the extreme autonomy of the German universities could permit professors living in the centre of Europe [...] to expound Liberal ideas to their students. Thus, when, owing to government pressure, the freedom of teaching was here and there violated, the universities became centres and hotbeds of revolt. The most famous example is the protest of the historian Dahlmann of Göttingen, which bore the signatures of the brothers Grimm, Gervinus, Eduard Albrecht, and others, against the Hanoverian government in 1837 on its violating the constitution it had sworn to respect. The protest was the more significant in that not only the liberty of the university but that of the country at large was at stake [...]. The seven professors who signed the protest were expelled from their chairs; but the people of Göttingen, mindful of the Liberalism which they had learnt to value under English government,

Many of them began by advancing reforms in the educational system to arrive at a scheme for wider social changes. This was the case with, for example, C.W. Rotteck, who started his career of a liberal as a defender of traditional university liberties and next became known as an advocate of civil rights in the Frankfurt parliament.

One of the first liberals to follow such a path in Prussia was Karl Wilhelm von Humboldt (1767–1845). He was a scientist, politician and reformer of the educational system at all levels. As Minister of Education, in 1810 he contributed to the establishment of the University of Berlin (which bears his name to today). In 1816, he was appointed Minister of Internal Affairs. However, in 1819 he was removed from this position under the charges of professing liberalism. In his writings, he opted for monarchism as well as constitutionalism. The principles of the latter are outlined in his *Memorandum Concerning the State Constitution of Prussia* (1818). There he postulated handing over many spheres of social life to local authorities and allowing common citizens to exercise more power in the running of the state. He justified these recommendations as follows: "through participation in legislation, administration and organization, the citizen will more consciously manifest his sense of citizenship and his civic skills, and thanks to this he will become more ethical and will attach a higher value to his actions and his individual life by connecting both these spheres more closely with the good of his fellow citizens."[8] He expected the constitution to include clearly stated provisions for the personal security of citizens, the protection of private property and the freedom of conscience, speech and the press. The *Memorandum* states that the role of the state is not the welfare of citizens (this was their own obligation), but safeguarding that they would not act against each other and protecting them from external threats. He considered excessive care of the state to be harmful to the state as well as its citizens.[9]

---

opened a public subscription on their behalf." G. de Ruggiero, *The History of European Liberalism*, Boston 1959, pp. 241–242.

[8] K.W. von Humboldt, *Denkschriften über Preussens Verfassung* [Memorandum Concerning the State Constitution of Prussia], in B. Sobolewska, M. Sobolewski (eds.), *Myśl polityczna XIX i XX w. Liberalizm* [Political Thought of 19th and 20th Century. Liberalism], Warsaw 1978, p. 246.

[9] He writes that in such an "overprotective" state "it is not so much the individual members of a nation living united in the bonds of a civil compact; but isolated subjects living in relation to the State, or rather to the spirit which prevails in its government – a relation in which the undue preponderance of the State element tends already to fetter the free play of individual energies. [...] In proportion as State co-operation increases in extent and efficiency, a common resemblance diffuses itself, not only through all the agents to which it is applied, but through all the results of their activity." He also adds that "as each individual relies upon the helpful vigilance of the State, he learns to abandon to its responsibility his fate." Cf. W. von Humboldt,

Karl vom Stein (1755–1831) was another political activist during the reign of Frederick William III. At the time of the Napoleonic wars he held numerous high offices in the Prussian government: in 1804 he was appointed Minister of Finance and Economy, and in 1807 he became the Prime Minister. During that period he implemented numerous reforms in the spirit of liberalism. For instance, he abolished serfdom, granted home rule to cities and imposed a law allowing the nobility to trade (previously, this was punished by the removal of noble privileges). His imprudent note suggesting the possibility of an anti-Napoleonic uprising became the direct cause of his dismissal (1808). He found refuge first in Austria and later in Russia (as a political advisor to Tsar Alexander I). After the Congress of Vienna, he withdrew from active political life. He spent his last years as a publisher and researcher (he published and was the editor of the periodical *Monumenta Germaniae Historica*).

In his "Political Testament," written while he was Prime Minister, he opposed class society and advocated providing opportunities for action to those who not only have their own welfare at heart, but also the welfare of their own nation. He writes here that "we should get rid of disharmony present in the nation, eliminate class struggle which makes us unhappy, create legal opportunities for every individual in the nation to be able to develop their own moral strengths and in this way make the nation love the king and the homeland and eagerly sacrifice for them their possessions and life."[10] Doubtless, he was a supporter of the kind of monarchism which takes into account the nation's will and concerns itself with giving the nation the possibility of expressing its will through its representatives: "My plan, thus, was to give the right of representation to every active citizen, no matter if he has one hundred drags or only one, if he is a farmer, manufacturer or a tradesman, if he is a middle-class worker or is spiritually linked with the state."

After the short period in which the liberal vom Stein held the Prime Minister's office in Prussia, more reactionary politicians took up the leadership. Not everyone, though, was a conservative or conservative sympathizer. Some of them, more or less directly, put liberal ideas into effect. This was the case with vom Stein's successor, the chancellor Carl August von Hardenberg (1750–1822). His undertakings included the confiscation of Evangelical and

---

Über die Grenzen der Wirksamkeit des Staates [On the Limits of State Action], Nuremberg 1946, p. 37 ff. In his commentary, Zbigniew Rau emphasizes that in Humboldt the wealth of liberal thought "was replaced by a postulate of an individual's self-improvement from which results another, as it were, extraneous one: a postulate of the country's respect for this self-improvement by renouncing most of its actions." Cf. Z. Rau, *Liberalizm. Zarys myśli politycznej XIX i XX wieku* [Liberalism. An Outline of Political Thought in the XIX and XX Centuries], Warsaw 2000, p. 50.

[10] Ibidem, p. 252 ff.

Catholic properties, the abolishment of guild restrictions and the introduction of legal regulations allowing peasants to become owners of the land they cultivated.[11] King Frederick William III was also fairly open to liberal ideas. He played a part in making Prussia resist Metternich's anti-liberal pressure and became the main initiator of Germany's unification – at first with regard to customs (in 1828 Prussia governed the creation of the Customs Union with Hesse-Darmstadt, which was joined in 1829 by Bavaria, Württemberg, Hanover, Hesse-Kassel, Saxony and a few other countries), and later in other fields.[12] In 1840, when Frederick William IV became the King of Prussia, the changes in this country had already gone so far that, despite his conservative ideas, he could do little to put them into effect.[13] In addition, the events abroad were not favourable to him, especially the wave of revolutionary manifestations in 1848. He was so terrified by them indeed that he issued a proclamation "To My Beloved Berliners," in which he promised to pardon political prisoners and convene the United *Landtag* (State Parliament). When all this turned out to be insufficient for his subjects (who, for instance, manifested their discontent in front of the king's palace), he appointed a liberal sympathizer, Ludolf Camphausen (1803–1890) as Prime Minister.

In other German countries in the first half of the 19th century, liberals and liberal ideology followed variegated paths. The relatively least resistance to liberal ideology was in central (such as Hesse-Homburg and Thuringia) and southern countries (e.g. Württemberg). From these regions emerged the most influential group of German liberals – such as the aforementioned initiator of the professors' revolt Carl W. Rotteck. They played a significant role in establishing in Frankfurt am Main (the seat of the German Union Parliament) the so-called preparatory parliament (Vorparlament, March 1848) and next (on May 18th) the German National Assembly, the country's representative

[11] "Hardenberg wanted to be even more accommodating with peasants, but he could not ignore the conservative opposition. In any case, serfdom was abolished, and from then on granges, substantially enlarged, had to rely on hired hands." J. Krasuski, *Historia Niemiec* [The History of Germany], Wroclaw – Warsaw – Cracow 2004, p. 169.

[12] "Twenty years later outside the German Customs Union remained only Austria, Lichtenstein, Mecklenburg-Schwerin, Mecklenburg-Strelitz, Holstein and 3 Hanseatic port towns: Bremen, Hamburg and Lübeck." Ibidem, p. 183.

[13] Guido de Ruggiero calls Frederick William IV a "belated Romantic, moved by the contradictory desires for a revived medievalism and a legitimatistic assertion of the divine right of kings." In front of the Prussian government he said: "No power on earth shall ever persuade me to exchange the natural relation between prince and people for a contractual and constitutional relation; or to countenance the insertion, between our Lord in Heaven and this country, of a piece of written paper, like a second providence, to rule by its paragraphs [...]." Cf. G. de Ruggiero, *The History of European Liberalism*, op. cit., p. 243.

body elected in general and free elections, a competitive force to the Prussian National Assembly (convened in Berlin at almost the same time, that is on May 22nd). Although the members of the Frankfurt parliament were active predominantly during internal conflicts and "academic" orations (223 speakers, including 88 professors, took the floor during an 8-day debate), and the parliament has been remembered as a symbol of unproductive garrulousness, it nevertheless managed to pass (on March 28th, 1849) the democratic constitution of the German Reich and entrusted Frederick William IV with uniting Germany.[14] The Prussian parliament decided, however, to pass the Frankfurt constitution, which resulted in the king's decision to dissolve its lower house and suspend the upper one. Other rulers of German countries, including the king of Württemberg, were also against passing the document.

One of the co-creators of the constitution was Carl Wecker (1790–1869), a professor of law (first at the University of Cologne, next in Bonn and Freiburg im Breisgau), a close collaborator of Rotteck, with whom he prepared (in 1834–1843) the 15-volume *National-Lexicon: Encyclopaedia of the Political Sciences for People of all Stations*, which was an explication of German liberalism in the first half of the 19th century. He was also a member of parliament (from 1831) of the Baden State Parliament and the National Assembly in Frankfurt (he belonged to the fraction of professors called "The Mess"). In *The National-Lexicon* he opted for "the community constituted freely from free citizens. Within it, particular individuals and their free unions are given at first a special, sanctified set of private rights in order for them to be able to exist within it as free and autonomous people and fulfil their convictions and purposes. Next, as free citizens and members of the governed organized community (the so-called civic society), they will be granted their own set of rights, their rightful and due status and position in communes, provinces, and representational assemblies together with the related rights in the field of civil liberties in order to implement and represent their private, political, and constitutional rights with regard to the government." He adds that "the government of a free or law-abiding state must acknowledge the governed nation united in one social body as an independent legal personality, not merely as a crowd devoid of any rights." In such a state, political opposition plays a major role: "It has been proved to be perfectly natural, unavoidable and salutary that in every state, especially in a free class system, the government or ministerial party and an oppositional party emerge and confront each other. Firstly, they make possible the fullest and most orderly representation and fulfilment of the two main courses of

[14] Frederick William IV was also offered the emperor's crown, but he refused, explaining that this dubious (to him) gift comes from the commonalty and not from his equals, i.e. other kings and princes.

state life, that is unity and freedom, conservation and progress. Secondly, they allow the perpetual and a most attentive examination of all state decisions as well as the disclosure of their one-sidedness and faults."[15]

Welcker's party was not the most liberal in the Frankfurt parliament. The members of the so-called Greater German Party went much further. They prepared their own project of the Reich Constitution. It included sections on all class privileges, the availability of public offices to all who possessed the right qualifications, every German's right to freely express their convictions in speech, writing and print, to the full freedom of religion and conscience, and a section on the ultimate abolishment of "all relations of dependence and serfdom," of "patrimonial fruit-growing and the landowners' police together with licenses and obligations resulting from these rights."[16]

3. Liberalism in the second half of the 19th century

The suppression of the social revolt known as the Springtime of the Peoples led to a complicated political situation for all forces, including the liberal one, which strove for fundamental social transformations. In many countries, the rulers (holding their positions "by the grace of God") felt strong enough to disregard the opposition and give executive power to strongly conservative politicians. A case in point can be Austria, where at first prince Felix Schwarzenberg (1800–1852) was Prime Minister. After his death the office was formally taken by the emperor himself, but in actual fact the Prime Minister was the Minister of Internal Affairs Alexander von Bach (1813–1893) – in his youth a liberal sympathizer, but determinedly opposed to it while being a high government official. In terms of internal policy, these two politicians became those who intensified repressions towards the opposition (the former "made his contribution" by reinstituting censorship, and the latter abolished the constitution of March 4th, 1849). What is more, they strengthened Austria's position abroad (mainly at the cost of Prussia in the German Union).[17]

[15] C. von Rotteck, C. Welcker, *Staatslexikon, Encyklopedie der samtlichen Staatswissenschaft* [The National-Lexicon: Encyclopedia of the Political Sciences for People of all Stations], vol. 12, in B. Sobolewska, M. Sobolewski (eds.), *Myśl polityczna XIX i XX w....* [Political Thought of 19th and 20th Century...], op. cit., p. 274 ff.

[16] Cf. ibidem, p. 288 ff.

[17] "Minister Bach expanded the police force, tightened censorship and rationalized bureaucracy whose aim was still to Germanize the state, and that is why higher administrative posts in the Czech State, Galicia and Hungary were taken by Germans." Cf. J. Krasuski, *Historia Niemiec* [The History of Germany], op. cit., p. 208.

The fact that Austria ignored public expectations – both in the member states of the empire and those under its influence – mobilized the Austrian opposition as early as at the end of the 1850s and forced the Vienna government to make concessions. One of them was appointing the post of Prime Minister to a middle-of-the-road liberal, Anton von Schmerling (1805–1895), and undertaking political system reforms (though with the centralist structure left intact). These changes turned out to be sufficient for economic strengthening of the country, but insufficient for allowing it to remain "the main player" among the German-speaking countries.

In only a few dozen years, Prussia took over the dominant position, and its leadership was confirmed when it succeeded in the unification of Germany in 1871. While attempting to achieve this, the Berlin authorities gained the support of the public opinion in the German countries through their prudent interior policy (e.g., they did not conform to conservatives appealing for the restoration of censorhip in Prussia, where it was abolished in 1849) and its firm and skilful foreign policy. First (in 1865), they defeated Denmark (in coalition with Austria), which held power in Schleswig and Holstein, and next (in 1866) they triumphed over Austria, which controlled the German Union and finally (in 1871) over France, which was in possession of Alsace and Lorraine.

One of the originators of this success was Otto von Bismarck (1815–1898). He was Prime Minister for almost 28 years (from 1862 to 1890) – first of the Kingdom of Prussia and next of the German Reich (together with the King of Prussia as the hereditary German emperor). While Bismarck has been one of the most widely discussed political figures, he was definitely not a liberal and far from cherishing any sympathies towards liberalism. As a steadfast conservative, more often than not he made life difficult for liberals in the parliament. However, at the same time he was a pragmatist and in the name of his highest aim, which for him was the Reich, he knew how to cooperate with them. And this is what he did with regard to religious issues and formal-legal decisions concerning the social status of the churches (he supported the solutions which limited their influence in education and politics).

None of the then eminent political forces denied that the Reich should be a state of law or a law-abiding state, which in fact stood for the same thing. It was debatable, however, what exactly this should mean. One of the first liberals to undertake an in-depth reflection on the state of law was Robert von Mohl (1799–1876). The term appears even in the title of his dissertation *Das Staatsrecht des Konigreiches Wurttenberger* [State of Law in the Kingdom of Württemberg, 1829]. Here he points out that although in every case such a state is bound up with the representational system, this system is differently understood and applied in various countries. The differences between the

United Kingdom and continental Europe are especially distinct. In the UK, the power belongs entirely to elective representational bodies (council and legislative ones), whose scope and method of action is defined by the positive law. On the other hand, for the Continent, including German countries, "the state power in the full meaning of the term and to the fullest extent belongs to the hereditary prince by their particular birth right. Although the execution of this power is limited not only by the positive regulations of a given local legislation, but also, and most importantly, by the basic rules of the law-abiding state, yet within those limits and this scope he acts exclusively according to his own convictions. As a result, the only task of civil servants is implementing the will expressed by the head of state and because of this, with the exception of the judiciary's independence [...], they do not realize any sovereign line of action both in terms of the overall shape of state affairs as well as particular problems."[18]

The term "the state of law" ("der Rechtsstaat") appears also in the dissertation by Rudolf von Gneist (1816–1895) entitled *Verwaltung, Justiz, Rechtsweg: Staatsverwaltung und Selbstverwaltung nach englischen und deutschen Verhältnissen mit besonderer Rücksicht auf Verwaltungsreformen und Kreisordnungen in Preussen* [Administration, judiciary, courts: State administration and self-government under British and German standards, with special attention to administrative reforms and county regulations in Prussia, 1882]. Gneist was a lawyer and politician, and member of the National Liberal Party, established in 1866. At first, it operated only in Prussia, but later encompassed the entire Reich. Gneist represented the party in the Prussian parliament (1859–1893) and the Reichstag (1867–1884), i.e. the Reich parliament.[19] He devotes one of the chapters of his work to a critique of the political system in contemporary France. In general, he accuses it of favouring politicians in lieu of the state of law. As a consequence, the government is unstable, administration embroiled in political games, bureaucracy is excessively expanded and legislative bodies are slaves to public opinion. He contrasts this system with the concept of the state of law: "the foundation-stone of the *Rechtsstaat* consisted in self-govern-

[18] R. von Mohl, *Staatsrecht, Völkerrecht und Politik* [State Law, International Law and Policy], vol. 1, in B. Sobolewska, M. Sobolewski (eds.), *Myśl polityczna XIX i XX w.*... [The Political Thought of the 19th and 20th Centuries...], op. cit., p. 466 ff.

[19] As the Constitution of April 16th, 1871 stated, the Reich was a federation, comprised of 4 kingdoms, 6 great principalities, 12 principalities and 3 free cities. All of them had a considerable autonomy with regard to internal policy and could even maintain foreign relations. Their governments had their representatives (their number depended on the size of a given part of the Federation) in the Federal Council (Bundesrat), which was an advisory as well as decision-making body (no bill could be passed without its approval). The only minister of the Reich was the chancellor.

ment, understood not as the participation of the people in a legislative and governing parliament, but as the possession by local bodies of governmental functions conferred upon them by the general judiciary, administrative, and financial laws of the State."[20] Such a state was also supported by the German Progress Party, established in 1861. In the Prussian parliament it demanded "a strong liberal government which sees its power in respecting the constitutional rights of citizens and is able to provide unconditional respect for these rules in all strata of the civil servants' world." With regard to legislature, the party opted for "the strict and consistent realization of the law-abiding state in accordance with the constitution."[21]

A controversial figure among the German liberals of the discussed period is Heinrich von Treitschke (1834–1896), a politician and scientist, lecturer at universities in Leipzig, Freiburg im Breisgau, Cologne, Heidelberg and Berlin. In concord with his party affiliations, his political views evolved from right-wing liberalism to conservatism. In Reichstag, where he was an MP in 1871–1884, he first was a member of the National Liberal Party and then of the German Conservative Party. While still considered a liberal, he became known as a supporter of a united Germany, with Prussia as the executive

[20] Cf. G. de Ruggiero, *The History of European Liberalism*, op. cit., p. 254 ff. Ruggiero draws attention to the fact that Germany – similarly to England – had a centuries-old tradition of self-government. It was upset by the collapse of the feudal system accompanied by the loosening of bonds with the Church and deepening the divide between nobility, burgeoisie and peasantry. Bismarck's administrative reforms are – according to Ruggiero – a successful attempt at restoring this tradition as well as adjusting it to the new social situation: "Bismarck brought about a great administrative reform based on self-government. Between the feudal party which wanted autonomous administration, but of a patrimonial type and in its own interest, and the Liberal *bourgeois* party, which meant by self-government a communal elective administration [...], Bismarck succeeded in finding a middle path, reconciling the old territorial interests with the new industrial and commercial interests of the *bourgeoisie*. His reform was based on the principle that the classes, in the modern sense of the term, must accept the task of personally discharging those public duties for which our times provide far more opportunity than any previous age. In modern conditions, it is impossible to get rid of the salaried State employee; but it is possible to supplement the rigid bureaucratic system at certain decisive points by calling in the help of the classes. Side by side with salaried officials, a system of unpaid officials can provide a juridical check on the administration, and at the same time train the educated classes in the practical exercise of political functions and so restore to them their lost legal consciousness." Ibidem, p. 256.

[21] "Owing to this we demand first of all the protection of the law by truly sovereign judges and the right for defense available equally to everyone. Pursuant to this, we demand the liquidation of the monopoly for bringing indictments by the non-independent public prosecution service [...], and finally the restoration of jurors' competences in cases concerning political and press offenses." B. Sobolewska, M. Sobolewski (eds.), *Myśl polityczna XIX i XX w....* [The Political Thought of the 19th and 20th Centuries...], op. cit., p. 461.

force and the House of Hohenzollern as the ruling dynasty. In "Prussische Jahrbücher" [the Prussian Yearbook] he promoted the view that in the name of national aspirations, the united Germany can and even should use every means available, including military force. In fact, he made a direct appeal for declaring war on France and taking from it such historical German regions as Alsace and Lorraine. He believed that it is not always necessary to take the most drastic steps, but all undertaken actions must be realized with absolute consistency. This was the way in which he supported – both by speeches and his pen – the policy of "Kulturkampf," i.e. the fight for a culture independent from the influence of the Catholic Church (but dependent on the national state). In his speech delivered in 1871 in Reichstag, he accused the Church that it "usurps the right to be the judge of political issues."[22] He did not, however, propose to completely oust clergy from politics. On the contrary, he thought that they ought to concern themselves with "the affairs of this world" but first of all, these had to be affairs of their own nation; secondly, clergymen should "in their own way sanctify and ennoble political life;" thirdly, they should talk about it "with care and moderation," and, fourthly, the state had to legally delimit the borders which the Church should not cross.

When he moved to the conservative side, he became less interested in fighting against the Church than with his former fellow party members. He reproached them for such "deadly sins" as "their spirit of hostility towards the state," "excessive individualism," "fanatical adherence to freedom," and such lesser misdeeds as "verbosity" or "doctrinairism." ("The man who thinks that the external mechanism of the vote can create a true liberty is a mere radical doctrinaire.")[23] It has to be added that while criticising liberals from the conservative position, Treischke did not share their view that at that time the Reich was not a liberal country. On the contrary, he thought it even more liberal than France or England. Proof of this was the freedom of speech, manifesting itself in, for instance, parliamentary debates and criticism of the administration.[24] The view that the Reich at the end of the 19th century was a liberal country is expressed also by some present-day historians.[25]

[22] In this way "the greatest achievement of the Reformation from 300 years ago is being questioned, that is the maturity of the state, its independence from the Church, its right to govern itself according to its own will..." Cf. ibidem, p. 472.

[23] Further discussion on this critique of liberalism can be found in G. de Ruggiero, *The History of European Liberalism*, op. cit., p. 262 ff.

[24] According to him, "[...] there is no State in Europe in which the parliamentary criticism of administration is so strict or so honest as in Germany." Ibidem.

[25] One of them is Jerzy Krasuski. In his *Historia Niemiec* [The History of Germany], he states that "although Germany's political system was not a full parliamentary democracy, it still was – like Prussia – a liberal and strictly law-abiding country, not worse in this respect than the

4. Liberalism in the Wilhelmian Epoch

In the history of Germany, the period from the end of the 19th century until 1918, which was the time of William II's rule (1888–1918), is called the Wilhelmian epoch. During these years the Reich underwent numerous changes with regard to social life and politics. The most important was the end of Bismarck's government. The Reichstag elections on February 20th, 1890, turned out to be the proverbial "nail in his coffin." Voters expressed their significant support for his political adversaries: the Catholic Center (106 seats out of 397 possible) and the socialists (in spite of the fact that antisocialist acts were repealed right before the elections, including the ban on forming any socialist organizations and assemblies). Liberals were also quite successful. Although the liberal right lost, the liberal left gained. However, these results were not enough to exercise a decisive influence on the Reich's politics.

When Bismarck stepped down on March 20th, 1890, a conservative general, Leo von Caprivi (1831–1899), became the chancellor and commenced the so-called "new direction." For foreign policy this meant a gradual departure from the alliance with Russia and the development of a closer relationship with the Great Britain. In terms of internal policy, it aimed at relieving social tensions through supporting industrial production (at the expense of farming). Unable to find sufficient backing for such a policy in the Reichstag, von Caprivi decided to call new elections (1893). This made his political opponents even more powerful, which resulted in Caprivi's resignation. Liberals were also among the ones who lost out. Not only did their parties gain fewer seats, but, in addition, the liberal left suffered new splits.[26] The shift on the highest governmental positions resulted in more conservative politicians becoming chancellors (Carl von Stamm-Halberg and next Bernhard von Bülow) and William II obtaining the actual leadership in the government.

For the liberals, this meant entering the hard period of political opposition. Although they were successful at times (e.g., when managing to reject the act which forbade activities "affronting God and the Church"), in most cases they experienced failures and their political position in the Reich was gradually becoming weaker (as the Reichstag elections in 1907 confirmed).

United Kingdom or France. People were not exposed to any lawlessness of the government. The freedom of speech, public meetings, the press and association was secured." Cf. J. Krasuski, *Historia Niemiec* [The History of Germany], op. cit., p. 235.

[26] The National Liberal Party split into the Free-minded Union (Freisinnige Vereinigung) and the Free-minded People's Party (Freisinnige Volkspartei).

In order not to become political outsiders, they first joined the so-called "Bülow bloc" (which opposed the Catholic Center and social democrats) and later (in 1910) they formed an electoral agreement with the social democrats (against the so-called "black-and-blues," that is the Catholic clergy and nobility), but the final outcome of these coalitions was also negative. This was proven by the elections in 1912. The social democrats achieved the greatest success, gaining 110 seats (the liberal right got 45 and the united liberal left 42). Their gravest failure, however, similarly to all other progressive forces in Germany, was their inability to oppose William II's imperial policy which in the short run improved the Reich's economic situation, but in the long run became one of the major reasons for the outbreak of World War I.[27]

At that time in Germany, there were liberals who not only showed no opposition towards this policy and ideology, but also more or less consciously supported them in their pronouncements. One of them was Friedrich Naumann (1860–1919). In 1907–1910 he was an MP in the Reichstag – first as a member of the Free-minded Union, and next of the Free-minded People's Party. In his *Das Prinzip des Liberalismus* [Principles of Liberalism, 1905], he contrasts the old liberalism with the new one. About the former he writes that "it was brave as a lion in fighting for the state to give freedom to individuals in order to make them unimpeded in using their hands and brains," and, as "a reformatory movement," it accepted two basic rules: "1. The state is all of us; 2. The state cannot do everything. [...] Thanks to these two rules the state has undergone a transformation. Its former omnipotence has been overcome, the individual spirit freed itself from the clutches of the state, but in our economic life there emerges a new omnipotence, the omnipotence of great companies, and against this new power we should again use the old method. Old liberal rules must now be reformulated: 1. The company is all of us; 2. The company cannot do everything." These old rules were to be championed not only by liberals under the reign of Frederick William IV, but also by later ones (such as, for instance, Ludwig Bamberger).[28]

The new liberalism was not only a shift in emphasis from the state to companies, but also "a full awareness" of man's material needs ("we go together

[27] In his discussion on the ideology which underlied this policy, Jerzy Krasuski writes that William II claimed that "Germany was powerful and deserved obedience in the whole world, that no one anywhere could do anything without Germany's consent and without any benefit for Germany arising from it. No German questioned this rule." Ibidem, p. 301.

[28] L. Bamberger (1823–1899) was a right-wing liberal. Until 1880, he was a member of the National Liberal Party (and he became this party's MP in the Reichstag in 1871). He was against Bismarck's expansionist policy and his attempts to introduce customs protectionism.

with the pressure of the masses towards a decent human existence").[29] Naumann's kind of liberalism meant also sensitivity to national issues, the pride of being a German and of acting for the greatness of Germany. In his *Principles of Liberalism* he writes: "Thanks to our character we, Germans, have something to give to the world. Because of its specificity, our culture has to occupy the deserved place in the history of humankind. Our German nation must aspire to win power. [...] Old German democracy believed that Germans have a great obligation to be an example to the world. This faith is not gloating, because we respect all others, but we also respect ourselves and we are not going to let ourselves be humiliated if someone wanted to push us aside into the recesses of world history. We are proud not because of what has been achieved, but of the fact that we are imbued with the desire for achieving whatever possible as a nation, whatever we can, in order to provide humanity with the refinement, originating from the depths of our German soul, for the development of humanity's thoughts and wants, for its art and work." Naumann's political activity makes it ascertainable that he was far from nationalist chauvinism.[30] However, in the Wilhelmian epoch, these words could and probably were interpreted as such.

At that time, German liberals continued to debate the concept of the law-abiding state. One of the most distinguished of its supporters was Georg Jellinek (1852–1911), a lecturer in the philosophy of law and politics at universities in Vienna and Heidelberg. In his *Allgemeine Staatslehre* [General Science of the State, 1900], his assumption was that all laws are conferred by the state. However, what has to be distinguished are private and public laws. The former (defined by him with the use of the Latin word *licere*) are of a primary character and are independent from man's personality, while the latter (defined by the word *posse*) depend on personality and, as a consequence, determine the

[29] Translating it into the rules of social policy, F. Naumann claims that "at the cost of maintaining itself, liberalism must firmly support industrial legislation, the freedom of public meetings, collective agreements, protection of workers – everything that increases the value of an individual among civil servants and workers." Cf. F. Naumann, *Die Politik der Gegenwart* [The Present Policy], in B. Sobolewska, M. Sobolewski (eds.), *Myśl polityczna XIX i XX w....* [The Political Thought of the 19th and 20th Centuries...], op. cit., p. 484 ff.

[30] During World War I, he advocated the idea of the so-called "Mitteleuropa." His dissertation bearing the same title and published in 1915 presented the vision of the federation of the Middle and South European countries, which should nevertheless be dominated by Germany. After the war, he established the German Democratic Party, the predecessor of today's Free Democratic Party (Freie Demokratische Partei – FDP) and remained its chair until his death.

specific status of an individual or – which amounts to the same – delineate the individual's sphere of independence from the state. In the law-abiding state, however, this independence is not absolute, but relative.[31]

[31] In his discussion on this concept, Guido de Ruggiero points out that "according to jusnaturalism the individual's original rights [...] are purely privatistic in nature; and therefore the public rights based upon them are rooted in private rights. It is enough to recall the doctrine of the social contract. This whole system of ideas is reversed by modern juridical thought. Not only are subjective rights consisting in a *posse* strictly public; but even those consisting in a *licere*, that is to say private rights, are based in the last resort upon public right. Jellinek actually restricts this principle to the limitation of rights of *licere* (for example, the limitation of the right of property on grounds of public interest [...]." Cf. G. de Ruggiero, *The History of European Liberalism*, op. cit., p. 261 ff. In contrast, Zbigniew Rau stresses that in the light of this concept, public laws "are both rights and obligations, so they do not allow for the recognition of any unconditional individual rights in the public sphere." Cf. Z. Rau, *Liberalizm...* [Liberalism...], op. cit., p. 94.

Chapter 4

Italian liberalism

1. Precursors

Various reasons caused the very dynamic and, during the Renaissance, influential culture of the Italian republics and principalities to show signs of stagnation in the second half of the sixteenth century and even regression in the seventeenth. Among the most important, undoubtedly, is fighting for the political and economic interests in the area by foreign countries – among others Spain, France and the German Empire.[1] Also of vital importance were the actions undertaken, after the Council of Trent, by the Church of Rome, which have passed into history as the "Counter-Reformation" or "Restoration." Leopold von Ranke writes that for all the members of this Church it meant "submitting their non-disposition to understand rigorism," which was guarded and enforced

[1] A good example would be the situation of the Venetian Republic. In the sixteenth century and even in the first half of the seventeenth century it belonged to the richest Italian states. However, the attempt by her patricians to obtain freedom from the foreign hegemony ended in disaster for her. First, the defeat suffered in the war with Ottoman Porte (1669) forced her to seek an ally in Vienna (accession to the so-called Holy League), and later the loss of markets in the Balkan peninsula caused her to become an element of the political game carried out by the Austro-Hungarian Habsburgs and to start to experience an economic crisis. The crisis also affected other Italian cities and states. Venice, which even in 1602 produced 29 thousand pieces of cloth a year, at the end of the century produced only 2 thousand; Milan, which at the beginning of the century had 60–70 companies operating in the wool industry, had 5 in 1682; Genoa at the same time experienced the reduction of turnover at her port from 9 to 3 million tons, and the number of silk weaving workshops from 18 thousand to 2.5 thousand; and Florence, which in the years 1560–1580 produced 20 thousand pieces of wool per year, in the middle of seventeenth century produced only 5 thousand." G. Procacci, *Historia Włochów* [The History of the Italian People], Warsaw 1983, p. 217.

by inquisitorial courts.[2] The political and cultural position of the larger and smaller Italian States was weakened by the exuberant ambitions of not only the old aristocratic families (the Medici family in Florence, the Este in Ferrara et al.), but also by the new families occupying positions (as in the case of Milan's Sforza) who sought to replace the former, to say the least. The same historian of the papacy notes that already in the middle of the sixteenth century in Italy "everyone wanted to be called 'Master.'" In addition to all this, traditionalism was still deeply rooted in the culture of the Apennine Peninsula. Virgiglio Titone, characterizing the mentality of Italians at the turn of the seventeenth and eighteenth centuries, maintains that: "They were not able to listen to new slogans of their time, they clamped up and rejected everything that increased the gap between them and any new ways of thinking or their sacred cultural values."[3]

This does not mean, of course, that no Enlightenment news reached them or that it was not received with sympathetic interest. Works such as *The History of Charles XII* by Voltaire, *The New Heloise* by Rousseau or the *Encyclopedia* edited by Diderot and d'Alembert, translated into Italian, did appear in Italy.[4] In large urban centers – such as Milan or Naples – there emerged not only a peculiar fashion for reading the works of French authors, but also for reading and writing in French. The diaries of the famous adventurer Giacomo Casanova, dissertations on economics by Ferdinando Galiani, and Carlo Goldoni's literary works were also written in this language.

The authors of articles published in Milan's magazine "Il Caffe" (such as Pietro Verri for example), wrote in Italian. Cesare Beccaria (1738–1794), son of Milan's patrician, owed his intellectual skills, however, not so much to his education at a Jesuit college (after its completion, he said that they taught there

[2] "[...] alongside the Spanish Inquisition stood the renewed Roman Inquisition; all Protestant movements were suppressed with violence. At the same time, however, particularly strong in these countries were the currents of spiritual life, which were claimed by and which were subdued by renewed Catholicism. Secular rulers also stood on the side of the Church." L. Ranke, *Dzieje papiestwa w XVI–XIX wieku* [The History of the Papacy from the XVI to the XIX Centuries], vol. 1, Warsaw 1974, p. 436 ff.

[3] Further, he writes that even if the Italians of that period were able to doubt the teachings of the Church, this doubting "they kept to themselves or their friends and did not make an issue out of it because it would involve their moral sensibility." Cf. V. Titone, *La storiografia dell'illuminismo in Iltalia*, Milano 1969, p. 9 ff.

[4] How these works reached Italy is shown by, among others, the correspondence of the resident of Rome, Alessandro Verri, with his brother Pietro: "I haven't got the *Encyclopedia* yet" he wrote in a letter of December 1770, "but it is located about 12 miles from Rome. I have a way to smuggle it in. I brought it to Civita Vecchia, from there by various opportunities I bring it into the vicinity of Rome, and finally, in the carriage of some cardinal, it enters the city. That's exactly what I did with everything that I was getting from London." P. Hazard, *Myśl europejska w XVIII wieku. Od Monteskiusza do Lessinga* [European Thought in the 18th Century. From Montesquieu to Lessing], Warsaw 1972, p. 98.

"fanaticism and suppressing the development of human feelings"), but rather to reading the works of French authors (such as Montesquieu, among others). In 1764, he published a work *On Crimes and Punishments* [Dei delitti e delle pene]. The controversial judgments of the contemporary tribunals had become, for many enlightened people, the inspiration to become interested in issues of the functioning of the law, judiciary and prisons. For Milan's enlightened citizens, such "a disgrace" for the judiciary of the time was the trial conducted in the seventeenth century of the so-called "flatterers."[5]

In the *Treaty On Crimes and Punishments*, Baccaria is not limited, however, to indicating specific judicial errors, but tries to show both the historical source of the existing laws, as well as their contemporary conditions. In his opinion, these laws are a legacy of the "barbarian laws of ancient conquerors [...] established twelve centuries ago through the holding of power by the Prince of Constantinople (probably the Emperor Justinian) – and later intermingled with the rites of Lombards and dark interpretations."[6] However, by way of their use, a decisive role was played by the superstitions and humour of the judges. All this, of course, defies enlightened reason and the sense of justice.

In his work, Beccaria proposes a fundamental reform of criminal law. In his opinion, in applying the law, judges should be guided by the general principle of the greatest possible good for the greatest number of citizens. In the judicial process, torture should be banned and punishment should be proportionate to the social harmfulness of the crime. During a trial, for the first time the principle that the effectiveness of punishment is not determined by its severity but the certainty of bearing the responsibility for the crimes committed was clearly formulated. The demand for abolishing the death penalty also appears. He considers the penalty not only to be barbaric but also ineffective.[7] It should also be noted that Beccarii presented in his treaty what might be called the general theory of social life. At its core is the assumption that life is a constant struggle of human passions, and the larger the country, the harder it is to control them. "It is impossible – he wrote – to prevent chaos accompanying the universal struggle of human passions. It grows in proportion to the population and the mixing of private interests, which cannot be regularly directed towards public benefit. If you look at history, you will see that disorder increases with the borders of the empire and in the same proportion, the nation's feelings decrease."[8]

---

[5] Titon calls the judicial judgment passed in the trial "the most shameful triumph of the most superstitious vulgarity." Cf. V. Titone, *La storiografia dell'illuminismo...*, op. cit., p. 52 ff.

[6] Cf. C. Beccaria, *Dei delitti e delle pene*, Torino 1911, p. 19.

[7] Even Montesquieu in *The Spirit of the Laws* did not go so far with his postulates. Beccaria knew this work and, moreover, it was a source of inspiration for him.

[8] Ibidem, p. 21.

The Treaty on Crimes and Punishments earned its author recognition both in Milan and far beyond its borders. In 1766, the book was translated into French, and a little later it was published in English, German, Spanish and Dutch. In 1768, he was offered the Chair of Economics in Milan's Palatine School (which he directed for two years), and in 1771 became a member of the Supreme Economic Council of Milan. From this period of his life comes his *Elements of Public Economy* [Elementi di economia publica]; the first edition of which appeared in 1804. These also contain innovative ideas – concerning among others the social division of labour and the relationship between the standard of living and the number of people.

Among the precursors of Italian liberalism, we also find Vincenzo Cuoco (1770–1823). A native of Naples, where he graduated from law school, he practiced law in the years 1790–1798. After the occupation of the city by France, he joined the French army and tried (unsuccessfully) to get a job in the new administration. After the liberation of this region of Italy from French occupation, he was arrested, put on trial and convicted (in April 1800) to 20 years in exile. He first went to France and later to Savoy and Piedmont. The capture of Northern Italy by Napoleon's army enabled him to live in Milan. There he joined the "Redattore cisalpino" team, later transformed into the "Giornale italiano;" in 1803, he became its editor-in-chief. In this pro-French journal, he also published articles and reviews. Earlier, in 1801, his three-volume *Historical Essay on the Neapolitan Revolution of 1799* [Saggio Storico sulla Rivoluzione Napoletana del 1799] appeared. In the years 1804–1806, he published a series of papers titled: *Plato in Italy* [Platone in Italia].

The years 1805–1810 were a period of considerable change in Italy. It was associated with the war led by France with the third anti-Napoleonic coalition. After the victory of Napoleon in 1805 against the Austrian troops and the peace settlement with Austria in Pressburg (today's Bratislava), he practically took control of Italy's kingdoms, principalities and provinces. Milan became the capital of the Kingdom of Italy. Its nominal ruler (with the title of viceroy) was Eugène Beauharnais (Napoleon's stepson). For Cuoco, it was the period of efforts to secure a government job, first in Milan, but when they proved to be ineffective, then he went to the capital of the Kingdom, Naples, where he received a position in Sacro Real Consilio (it was a judicial institution). In 1807, he became a member of The Committee on Civil Code, and headed the Commission on Judicial Officers. These positions were associated with a significant salary and honours. Joachim Murat, sitting on the throne of Naples, was able to appreciate his pro-French commitment and not only presented him with awards, but also appointed him first (in 1809) as a member of the Committee for Educational Reform, and later (in 1812) as director of the Royal Treasury.

From this period of Cuoco's life come his writings concerning education, land reclamation and reforestation issues. He wrote a number of articles for "Corriere di Napoli" and "Monitore dell Due Sicilie."

Relatively, the most entangled in contemporary politics is his *Historical Essay*. Titone compares it to *Reflection on the Revolution in France* by Edmund Burke and *Considerations on France* [Considerations sur la France] by Joseph de Maistre. It is possible that Cuoco knew both works. However, in his *Essay*, he was not as critical towards those who first brought about the *French Revolution*, and later caused it to leave behind so many victims, such as his predecessors. First, he tried to explain these events by objective circumstances – different for France and the Kingdom of Naples. An example of these differences for him was the religious life in both countries. In the first country, there were many different sects, while the second country "was proud that there never appeared any sect nor heresy." In his opinion, they were not there not just because the inquisitorial courts worked so eagerly, but because its inhabitants exhibited "the lack of moral energy" needed for the spirit of rebellion, or change, to appear. Added to this was their inborn caution, no tendency to fanaticism and aversion to abstractionism – such was the case, in his opinion, not only in France, but also in England, and even in America. All this caused the Neapolitan revolution of 1799 to be unsuccessful – despite the fact that the ministers and generals in this kingdom were "inept and cowardly."

Both in this work and in articles printed in the "Giornale italiano," Couco preached the idea that you cannot do anything great without great men. In one of his articles, he claimed that "a nation that has no leaders quickly loses any significance whatsoever."[9] In *Plato in Italy*, he added that of little avail for the nation are the enlightened guides if the people are uneducated – at least they should be educated enough to understand the laws enacted by the former and to be able to respond to their potential errors.

The same idea appears in his six *Fragments of Letters to Vincezio Russo* [Frammenti di lettere dirette a Vincezio Russo] dating back to 1799. These notes were created in connection with the draft of the Constitution prepared by a member of the Republican Government in Naples, Mario Francesco Pagano (1748–1799).[10] Writing about the task of legislators, Cuoco concludes that their main goal should be to make the "nation feel happy and to love its happiness." Bold criminals are not the only obstacle to its implementation, but also simple and uneducated people, who have their own customs. Lawmakers must reckon

---

[9] Cf. V. Cuoco, *Scritti vari di V.C.*, Bari 1924, p. 29 ff.

[10] Arguing against the project, at the same time he believed its author was one of the most enlightened Italians at that time – about F. M. Pagano's work, he wrote (in *Plato in Italy*) that it is "one of the best books on the subject."

with them, just as they need to take into account local traditions in terms of governance and self-government. The weakness of Pagano's project, it turned out, was that he did not draw upon the latter, but on the French Constitution of 1795. He was not trying, of course, to duplicate those traditions, but to develop and enhance them, eliminating what was wrong in them. Among the harmful elements of Neapolitan tradition, he included the corruption occurring in government offices, centralization and the individualism of the inhabitants of this kingdom.

In his *Fragments*, he wrote, "I have crossed part of the Adriatic coast and there is hardly a single inhabitant who had not thought of creating a port [...], nor is there a single person who would one day not even start to build it." However, on the topic of centralism he wrote: "Since authorities settled into the municipal government, the public spirit cooled down. Management took care of everything, but wanting to do everything, they did not do anything, or did everything wrong." A prime example of corruption in the Kingdom of Naples was, for him, the construction of the roads. In his opinion, huge sums of money were spent on this purpose, but nothing was done because "architects and the tax officials devoured everything." One of the biggest weaknesses of the kingdom would be the fact that outside of Naples, there was no other major city ("the province is nothing more but a desert").[11]

In this treaty, he also presented his proposal for a political system. This system is called the "despotism of law" – we should add constitutional law. City authorities and the enlightened monarch should implement it. The task of the latter is – as indeed for every king in a constitutional monarchy – not so much governance, but the role of a mediator between various ambitious citizens and – which in this case, Cuoco considered especially important – "to eliminate or reduce the middle class of management officials, lawyers and writers." The social groups listed here he called "parasites of the kingdom" consuming "a fourth part of its wealth." In later years, he considered as such enlightened monarchs both Napoleon Bonaparte and, reigning by his will in the Kingdom of Naples, Joachim Murat.

Plato in Italy in its literary convention refers to accounts of travel popular at the time – such as, among others, *The Persian Letters* of Montesquieu in France.[12] The author is not present in this work in the role of a traveler, however, but as a reporter of a supposedly found Greek manuscript, consisting of letters between Plato and a young Cleobulus. In these letters, it appears that the ancient culture of the Italics (inhabitants of the Italian Peninsula) was

[11] Cf. ibidem, p. 223 ff.

[12] G. Natali suggests that as a model for this work served *Plato's Travels around Italy* by Fr. Eduardo Corsini. Cf. G. Natali, *Cultura e poesia in Italia nell'età napoleonica*, Torino 1930.

not only equal to Greek culture, but in many respects, it was superior to it. The fact that the later came to its collapse is the result of the same historical processes that were present in Greece, that is, the fighting of political factions and groups, the dominance of extreme views, and above all, devastating social ties due to "blind greed" – the "daughter of incontinence, prompting to view the neighbour not as a friend who can we help in need, but as a servant, from whom one demands to satisfy his whims and from whom first he steals his property, meaning his hands, and ultimately life itself."[13] Greed turns out to be, at the same time, the mother of the most devastating social plague to humanity – that is corruption – thanks to which "nobles became the oppressors, and the people became intolerant." In answering the question: how can this evil be remedied? Cuoco answers that first we need to discover the truth about human nature, then the truth about the Italian nation, and finally these truths must be made universal through properly conducted public education.

His suggestions on such education appear in both treaties mentioned here, as well as in written form at the request of Murat in the *Report on the State of Education in the Kingdom of Naples*. To a lesser extent he was interested in the related organizational and administrative issues, to more of the ideological, in particular national ones. In his opinion, public education should in general shape the spirit of work and professional activity ("the goal of knowledge is action"), and this, in turn, should be joined by the spirit of national pride from both the achievements of ancestors, and by what contemporary generations represent. In *Plato,* he admitted that he "admires the Italian customs as they express and fuel the strength of the spirit of ancestors." However, in one of the articles published in the "Giornale italiano," he stated, "The Italian exceeds or is on a par with the representative of any other nation." He claims that an Italian's main weakness is found in their lack of willingness or inability to unite with other Italians. In *Plato* he wrote: "if Italians are divided, they will fight until they exterminate each other. [...] If they are united, they will pass laws for the entire universe."

Titone, when analyzing Cuoco's educational program, draws attention to the existence of such modern elements as the demand for equal education for both men and women, the introduction of free public education (at the primary level), or its becoming independent from the Church – in the opinion of this author "Cuoco was a supporter of the separation of Church and State." However, his assessment of individuals persecuted by the Church was not unequivocal. This is confirmed by his comments about Giulio Cesare Vanini. In his *Historical Essay*, he wrote "the character of this man was special. It combined

[13] V. Cuoco, *Platon in Italia,* in idem, *Scritti vari di V.C.*, op. cit., p. 159 ff.

amazing ambition and cruelty. [...] Every case which he undertook was enormous, but he wanted to make it the greatest of all."[14] Cuoco's opinion about Vanini, not very flattering, Titone justified by Cuoco's aversion to extremes.

2. Radical liberalism during the Risorgimento

In the first decades of the 19th century, the ideas of the radical left were supported by some of the lower middle class and wageworkers, especially among the charcoal burners. They set up a secret society known as the Order of Charcoal Burners (Italian Carbonari – coal); its members called themselves "Good Cousins." Most likely, the first such organizations emerged in Calabria, and later in the Kingdom of the Two Sicilies and Piedmont (in the years 1820 to 1821 they caused the outbreak of the uprising there), Modena, Parma, and the Papal State. They sought to abolish the monarchy and to establish democratic republics. However, unlike the French Republicans, they did not reject the worship of Christ. On the contrary, they recognized Christ as the First Republican and as the victim of earthly tyrants. This was the reason that a large number of lower rank clergy was found among them. Its organizational structure was patterned after the Masonic lodges. The lowest organizational unit in this movement is the so-called "tent" (Italian *Vendita*), which in turn formed a provincial network, which also in turn combined into the "Supreme Tent of the World." In 1833, as an offshoot of this movement, the Charbonnerie démocratique was formed, which founded its own "Supreme Tent" in Paris. It represented the Italian variant of Jacobinism. It advocated, among others, far-reaching egalitarianism, and the confiscation of property from privileged social groups.[15] After 1848, operating in different countries, the Carbonari movement was absorbed by Freemasonry.

Giuseppe Mazzini (1805–1872) was also of Carbonari origin. He was one of the more radical Italian Liberals of the nineteenth century, and at the same time a person playing an important role in the Risorgimento (Italian for *Renaissance*), a national movement, which in the years 1820–1870 led to the eventual unification of Italy and the founding of an independent State.[16] He

---

[14] Cf. V. Cuoco, *Saggio storico sulla Rivoluzione napoletana del 1799*, d'Ajala 1861, p. 34 ff.

[15] M. Buonarroti was active first as a student in Pisa, then from 1790 published the radical magazine "Giornale Patriottico di Corsica" in Corsica, and from 1794, for the cause of Italy in Paris, first, he tried to win the Directorate, then Napoleon Bonaparte; in the opinion of the already quoted here Giuliano Procacci, "the cause of the Italian revolution and French Jacobinism were one and the same."

[16] According to Ruggiero, "the Italian Risorgimento is essentially a question of moral values: honour, justice, sacrifice, selflessness, loyalty." Cf. G. de Ruggiero, *The History of European Liberalism*, Boston 1959, p. 300.

was born in Genoa, in a middle-class family (his father was a doctor), and was already involved with the Carbonari movement during his studies of law at the local university (he graduated in 1827). After the unmasking of a conspiracy in Genoa, he was arrested and imprisoned in the fortress of Savona. After his release, he was ordered to leave Italy. He first settled in Marseille (there he founded a patriotic organization in 1831 called *Young Italy*), and later in London (where he published a newspaper "Apostolato Popolare").[17] In his publications, he endorsed the idea of the liberation of the Italian States from foreign domination and uniting them into one republic – not only free from foreign influence, but also implementing the freedoms written into the *Declaration of the Rights of Man and of the Citizen* (both that of 1789, as well as that of 1793). He presented the French Revolution as the culmination of the efforts of many generations undertaken over many centuries; with regard to the eighteenth century, he wrote, "it had its faith, its mission and practical programs for implementing them. It was a titanic work, with boundless faith in human liberty and power. Its mission was to compile [...] the assets of the first Epoch in the European world: to summarize and reduce to a specific formula that which eighteen centuries of Christianity examined, developed and made a fact: to create such an individual, described previously as – free, active, holy and inviolable; it was the mission of the century. The French Revolution achieved this [...]. The instrument for accomplishing a revolution and completing this mission was the law. Its strength, its mandate and the legal justification are based in the theory of rights; its most perfect expression was the *Declaration of Rights*."[18] It is not only an appraisal of the revolution, the revolutionaries and revolutionary methods, but also a manifestation of a total lack of sentiment towards this and those who found themselves on the other side of the barricade and who paid a high price for their defense of the *ancient régime*.

While living in London, Mazzini revived "Young Italy" (1839), and the organization began to recruit new members (mostly from among Italian workers living as migrants). However, in this regard he did not achieve much success, and the failure of the uprising started in Calabria in 1844 (headed by the Bandiera brothers cooperating with Mazzini) contributed to a decline in his

[17] On the pages of these magazines, he polemized, among others, with Carbonari Liberalism – which he accused of "not being able to see anything beyond humanity and individuality, ignoring the nation and society; it is utilitarian, not moral, and speaks only about rights and not duties." Cf. F. M. Adorno, T. Gregory, V. Verra, *Storia della filosofia*, vol. 3, Roma – Bari 1977, p. 407 ff.

[18] G. Mazzini, *Faith and the Future*, in B. Sobolewska, M. Sobolewski (eds.), *Myśl polityczna XIX i XX w. Liberalizm* [Political Thought of 19th and 20th Century. Liberalism], Warsaw 1978, p. 292 ff.

popularity (he was accused of sending to death inexperienced young people). The events of 1848, however (the so-called *Spring of Nations*) improved his situation immensely. Primarily, it was now possible for him to return to "Italy" and to get involved in direct political activity in this country. First he was active in Tuscany, and after the outbreak of the revolution in Rome (February 1849) he joined the local Republicans, and even stood at the head of the revolutionary government, leading the defense of the city besieged by, as requested by Pope Pius IX, the French army.

From this period came his most radical pronouncements. At this time, he argued, among other things, that "morality without freedom does not exist, because if there is no freedom to choose between good and evil, between dedication to universal progress and the spirit of selfishness, there is no responsibility. Without Freedom there is no real society because there can be no union between free men and slaves, but only one man ruling over another. Freedom is as sacred as the individual is sacred, for whom it constitutes the essence of life." However, appealing to all patriotic Italians, he claimed, among other things, that the task before them is to bring about "the unity of the nation in the material aspect, through the re-conquest of Trentino, Istria and Nicea, in the moral aspect through national education with free and protected teaching of each heterodox doctrine," the abolition of "all the offices that currently have as a goal representing the government's undue influence in various local districts," the introduction of the "universal right to vote as the beginning of political education," "the elimination of all obstacles limiting the free circulation of products inside and outside the country," the abolition of monopolies and the "introduction of legal responsibility for every Government official," etc.[19] It should be emphasized that Mazzini in his social philosophy did not deny the existence of God, nor the need by man to look for support from Him infighting for his rights as a citizen. On the contrary, in many cases he was persuading Italians that they have "no other master but God in heaven and no other Nation on earth." He added, however, that "no one has any right to persecution, intolerance or exclusive legislation in matters of their religious opinions. Nothing but the peaceful, great voice of humanity has any right to stand between God and your conscience." There is no doubt that the "nobody" and the "nothing" for him first of all meant the Pope and traditional Catholicism.[20]

---

[19] G. Mazzini, *On the Duty of Man and other Essays*, qtd. after B. Sobolewska, M. Sobolewski (eds.), *Myśl polityczna XIX i XX w.* ... [Political Thought in 19th and 20th Century...], op. cit., p. 489 ff.

[20] It is also underlined in the literature – when characterizing the so-called Mazzinism, Valerio Verra declares that traditional Christianity has already completed its mission: "the truth that was in it, that is, individual redemption, has already won;" what remains to be implemented

The defeat of the revolution of 1849 meant for Mazzini the necessity of another emigration. He moved to London again, and there first of all organized the association called Friends of Italy in 1851, and later the Central Committee of the European Democracy. In 1856, Mazzini secretly arrived in Genoa to directly control preparations for the next uprising. The failure of the armed revolt in Calabria in 1857 resulted in criticism of the methods of struggling for the liberation and unification of Italy endorsed by him and his *Action Party*. After the establishment of the Kingdom of Italy in 1861, he refused to join the forces that had led to it. In the last years of his life – criticized by both the right and the radical left – he completely withdrew from politics.

Carlo Cattaneo and Giuseppe Ferrari were among the critics of Mazzini at that time. They were also radical liberals, but in their radicalism, they did not favour revolution but organizational work and not just for one nation, but for all European nations. Characterizing their views, Valerio Verra writes, "Their radicalism comes face to face with traditional institutions and beliefs, undermining their value. Their guide is the light of science and reason. Science and education are the most important values, not recognizing any metaphysical or religious transcendence. [...] Cattaneo knows nothing about the specific missions of individual nations, although Ferrari is assigning democratic France the role of the power that initiates progress and change in Europe, and both of them are really interested in the free development of all individuals affiliated everywhere in a similar way."[21] In their writings – printed, among others, on the pages of Milan's "Annali di statistica" (published since 1832) – they spoke out against various forms of monarchical centralism and on behalf of republican federalism (in the Swiss or North American style).

3. Moderate Liberalism during the Risorgimento

Serious competition for the radical liberals during the Risorgimento was created by liberals forming the so-called "moderate party." One of them was Vincenzo Gioberti, a Piedmontese priest who called the Italians to moral revival and

is the essential belief in God who is leading humanity towards social unity; "as long as the social unity is not established, spiritual and political authorities must remain as much as possible independent of each other. When a new society will be established, this division between State and Church, the political and religious institutions, will no longer have the right to exist [...]; the State will be the Church, and the Church will be the State..." Cf. F. Adorno, T. Gregory, V. Verra, *Storia della filosofia*, op. cit., p. 410.

[21] "They do not want," writes the author "a homogenous nation encompassing the whole of Italy, because they consider it to be imposed from above and outside, to the detriment of the individual peoples of Italy." Cf. ibidem, p. 413 ff.

political unification in his work titled *The Civic* and *Moral Primacy of the Italians* [Il Primato morale e civile degli Italiani, 1843]. He introduced the concept of Italy as a federal state, where the Pope played the leading role.[22] Cesare Balbo refers to this work in a treatise titled *The Hope of Italians* (where he advocated, among other things, granting the roles of leadership in the future federation to the rulers of Piedmont) and so did Massimo d'Azeglio in his *Program for the Italian National Opinion* [Programma per l'opinione nazionale italiana, 1847]. A program of moderate liberalism was also presented by a group who first gathered around the magazine "Il Conciliatore," and later (after its liquidation) around "Anthology" published in Florence (where the position of leadership was held by Gino Capponi); there was also a group of journalists in Bologna established around Marco Minghetti (he advocated, among other things, constitutionalism, but one with considerable privileges for the Princes of Piedmont and Savoy).

The most prominent and the most influential figure among the "moderates" was count Camillo Benso Cavour, born in Turin (1810–1861). He came from a family with ties to the ruling house of Savoy. He held various offices, and remained loyal to them even after he became one of the main creators of Italian unification (Victor Emmanuel II, the representative of this house, received the Crown of the King of united Italy). Cavour had already encountered the ideas of liberalism during his studies in Turin Military Academy (at that time, among his friends was Baron Severino Cassio, well known for his republican beliefs). After a brief "career" at the court of Charles Albert, the Duke of Savoy and Piedmont, ending with a social scandal (reportedly he made fun of the required page's uniform), Cavour started training in the military Corps of Engineers. At that time, he met the members of the Carbonari movement and the supporters of Mazzini. Discouraged by the relationships prevailing in the army, he resigned from the army and took up the duties of mayor in a small town near Turin and as administrator on the estate belonging to his uncles.

The trip undertaken in the mid-30s to Paris, London and Geneva had a significant impact on his liberal beliefs (in the spirit of Constant's and Guizot's views). He began to publish in the pages of various newspapers (at that time he mainly spoke on economic affairs), and in 1848 founded his own journal – calling it "Il Risorgimento." He advocated, among other things, a constitutional monarchy and liberation from Austrian domination, but after the outbreak of the war with Austria, already as a member of the Piedmont parliament, he opted for a rapid conclusion of the peace agreement, which triggered an avalanche of criticism. Subsequent events had confirmed the need

[22] V. Verra emphasizes that in this work, "there are many backward and utopian elements" such as "leaving the fate of Italy and even the whole of European civilization in the hands of the Pope and the clergy."

to end the war, and prudent economic ideas still strengthened his position as a politician. In 1850, he first received the position of Minister of Agriculture and later Minister of Finance in the government of Massimo d'Azeglio. After the fall of the d'Azeglio's administration, King Victor Emmanuel II gave him the task of forming the government (1852). Moderate-minded politicians joined; nevertheless, they supported modernization, secularization and the unification of Italy under the leadership of Piedmont. His shrewd domestic politics and foreign policy (he gained the support of Emperor Napoleon III for the cause of Italy, among others) allowed, first, the military victory over Austria (of Solferino in 1859), and later led to the creation of the Kingdom of Italy (with its capital in Turin). Cavour died a few months after this event, and the work of unification was completed by other "Piemontese" (Venice was annexed to this kingdom in 1866, and in 1870, Rome).

Cavour's writings confirm that he was not only a careful politician, but also a philosopher of politics. Dear to him were the ideals of the French Revolution, but strange to him were both the spirit of the revolution, as well as the revolutionary methods for solving social problems. He stressed the need to reckon with stagnant tradition ("Respect and love for historical traditions which exemplify national glory are certainly sentiments worthy of the highest praise") which in Italian reality meant, among others things, respecting the traditions of the municipal authorities – such as, for example, the Signoria from the 12th to the 16th centuries. Cavour appealed for the resurrection of this "spirit of municipalism," and at the same time for making it the basis of constitutionalism. "City Councils," he wrote "do not have to be independent of political organs, and for this reason it is necessary to precisely separate the municipal laws, which should be administrative, from the political laws. This is an [...] essential condition for a wise constitutional system, which should seek to reconcile the freedoms of a nation with a strong and united central government."[23]

One of the main tasks of the progressive social forces was the adoption of the electoral law, which would allow for "the establishment of the Assembly, which would, as much as possible, in an honest and faithful manner represent the true interests, views and rightful feelings of the nation, and which must consist of citizens able to fulfill this difficult task, and yet possessing sufficient knowledge and ethics to usefully collaborate in legislating laws and managing the country." However, it was not supposed to be the law enacted by the majority of the nation, since this majority was composed of the uneducated

[23] C. B. Cavour, *De legge elettorale*, qtd. after B. Sobolewska, M. Sobolewski (eds.), *Myśl polityczna XIX i XX w....* [Political Thought in 19th and 20th Century...], op. cit., p. 299.

and impoverished masses. Cavour called such *Majority Rule* "one of the most dangerous sophisms of modern times," and he opposed it with the right of the minority – not only those educated enough to understand the true interests of the nation, but also wealthy enough "not to be easily forced to yield either to parties or to the government," and to be "interested in maintaining social order."

After analyzing various solutions, which in this regard were adopted in other countries, Cavour came to the conclusion that the most appropriate thing for Italy would be a mixed system, taking into account, as in France, the amount of paid "concession tax," and, as in England, an annual payment of rent from occupied locales, but these thresholds would be different not only in different regions, but also in different cities, because they had different economic and demographic situations.[24] For him, however, there was no doubt that "the greater the number of citizens who are able to participate in the elections, the greater the moral prestige of the mandate of the deputies and real power bestowed on them to resist the abuse of power by authorities as well as the excesses of the people."

Part of the Italian tradition, among other things, was the strong influence of the Catholic Church and the power of the Pope, which had to be reckoned with by the governments of the republics and principalities. For a liberal, this was not an easy problem to solve. It was particularly difficult for the liberal right in Italy, because, at the same time, it was attached to the Church and to the ideas that sought to limit its political influence. If we are to believe Marco Minghetti, who was closely working with Cavour and in the years 1873–1876 was the Prime Minister of the Italian Government, Cavour generally advocated for the separation of Church and state (the Vatican City was the only exception) and at the same time believed that it should "find itself in a position much higher than would result from the possession of a patch of territory and a handful of subjects." He had no bad intentions towards the head of the Church, such as, for example, to limit his spiritual independence. He stressed, however, that "consideration should be given to the traditions of the Italian Risorgimento, which from the very beginning established its purpose and limits: to overthrow the temporal power of the Pope; Rome as the capital; a free church in a free state..."[25]

---

[24] "It might be decided that the voters will be all those who occupy, for shops or workshops, premises with an estimated annual rent of about, in Turin and Genoa, 600 lire, and in other cities a lower amount, which would decrease depending on the number of citizens to 200 lire, and these limits should not be exceeded." Ibidem, p. 308.

[25] Cf. M. Minghetti, *Stato e Chiesa*, Milano 1878, qtd. after B. Sobolewska, M. Sobolewski (eds.), *Myśl polityczna XIX i XX w.* ... [Political Thought in 19th and 20th Century...], op. cit., p. 498 ff.

This corresponds well with the liberal ideology, but contrasts with the centuries old Catholic tradition. Hierarchs of the Catholic Church quickly figured it all out and, in 1866, there appeared the so-called "Roman Question." It boiled down to a declaration by Pope Pius IX of a vigorous dissent (*votum separatum*) against attempts to include Rome in the Kingdom of Italy. This led to a wave of anticlerical outbreaks and prompted the government to undertake a military expedition against Rome. The city was captured on September 20th, 1870, but the Pope refused to sign any treaty with the victorious Italy (even though it guaranteed his freedom, inviolability, and 3 million liras of annual compensation).

In the second half of the nineteenth century and at the beginning of the twentieth, the liberal right was one of the most important forces on the Italian political scene. It clashed with both conservatives as well as leftist liberals and socialists. Among its leading representatives were the Silvio brothers and Bertrando Spaventa. They became known as defenders of a strong state, yet such a state that does not serve the interests of only one party, but also upholds the rights of citizens, and leaves a number of public powers in the hands of elected local authorities. In assessing the political activities of these and other members of the liberal right, Guido de Ruggiero writes that, in general, "they followed the principles laid down by Cavour," introducing, however, a number of important amendments – among others a compromise in terms of the Church and State relations. Many of them were in favour of "agnosticism, or even an atheistic state," but there was no shortage of those who wanted to "make the State the universal center of religious life and pass on the tasks that every Church considers as its exclusive right."[26]

---

[26] Cf. G. de Ruggiero, *The History of European Liberalism*, op. cit., p. 324 ff.

Annex

The beginnings of liberalism in Poland

These beginnings – similarly, in fact, to other European countries – can be traced back to the second half of the 18th century and were influenced by the events taking place in Poland, at that time bearing the name of the Commonwealth of Both Nations (The Kingdom of Poland and the Grand Duchy of Lithuania). It was a geographically vast country (at the height of its territorial expansion it covered about one million square kilometres) going through at this time a serious crisis of power. The successive royal elections had revealed that the democracy of nobles (with the rule of *liberum veto*, which was derided in Europe) was incapable of providing the country with either a strong monarch or a responsible and competent executive power. This democracy was based on a system of variegated parliaments and assemblies: the general, executive, convocational, coronation and electoral ones. The latter were already functioning in the 15th century (for example, the elective method was used in the case of King Jan Olbracht), but the system of royal elections in the Polish Republic developed in the second half of the next century, and were established while the successive monarchs were elected. In the elective assembly, all the nobles had the right of vote and everyone with a knighthood could take part in electing the monarch (it was the so-called rule of *viritim*). The elections were valid when all voters opted for the same candidate. In practice, the participants of these assemblies formed elective groups from particular voivodeships and regions and then voted accordingly, with their stance previously agreed. Such a construction of the democracy of nobles resulted in the breaking up of all the common assemblies convened between 1736 and 1763.

The extent of Poland's deadly political sins was enhanced by the exuberant ambitions of magnates and Church hierarchs (including primates and papal nuncios). The situation was exacerbated due to the threat posed by the increasingly more powerful neighbouring countries (Russia, Prussia and Austria), the interference in Polish affairs of other contemporary powers and the deepening of economic difficulties resulting from the crisis of the grange-farm corvée economy as well as the wars ravaging the country, recurring crop failures, epidemics, etc. All this caused Poland to be perceived by foreigners as a country in the state of a serious downfall. One of them, William Coxe, wrote in his account of his visit to Poland in 1778–1780: "The present situation of the Polish nation impressed my mind with the most pathetic ideas of fallen greatness; and I could not consider, without a mixture of regret and sympathy, a people who formerly gave law to the North, reduced to such a low state of insignificance and domestic misery. The nation has few manufactures, scarcely any commerce; a king almost without authority; the nobles are in a state of uncontrolled anarchy; the peasants groaning under a yoke of feudal despotism far worse than the tyranny of an absolute monarch. I never before observed such an inequality of fortune, such sudden transition from extreme riches to extreme poverty; [...] the boasted Polish liberty is not enjoyed to the smallest degree by the bulk of the people, but is confined to the nobles or gentry."[1] The country could have been saved from oncoming disaster only by a miracle. This, however, did not happen and at the end of the 18th century, in 1795, Poland lost its political sovereignty.

Before this became a reality, however, there had been attempts to save the country. A significant contribution in this respect was made, among others, by King Stanisław August Poniatowski (1764–1795), a well-educated monarch (he knew a few languages) who clearly understood the needs of his own country. He was influenced by the ideas of the Enlightenment (especially the French enlightenment) and his political activities popularized them in the Polish Republic. He was an aristocrat by birth, but a democrat by conviction (in the style of the then English democracy). His achievements are quite numerous. The first one was the foundation of Szkoła Rycerska (the School of Knights) in Warsaw in 1765, and the last was signing of the government bill which in the history of Poland became known as the Constitution of the 3rd of May. In addition, he also openly supported the forces whose imperative was to save the country from anarchy and the parcelling out of it among predatory neighbours, as well as their attempt to elevate Polish society to a higher intellectual level. In order to realize the latter of these aims, in 1773 the king created the Com-

[1] Qtd. after G. L. Seidler, *W nurcie filozofii Oświecenia* [In the Mainstream of the Enlightenment], Lublin 1984, p. 223. Comp. W. Coxe, *Travels into Poland, Russia, Sweden, and Denmark: Interspersed with Historical Relations and Political Inquiries*, vol. 1, printed by J. Nichols, for T. Cadell, London 1784, p. 122.

mission of National Education. The significance of these actions for Poland was appreciated by foreigners visiting our country, many of whom praised the king. After he signed the Constitution of the 3rd of May, a journalist from the "Gazette of the United States," published in London, wrote: "In the history of humankind we can find few examples of kings who, not forced or threatened, would voluntarily agree to limit their own power. There are many apt sayings for momentous occasions, but we will find none to surpass the latest decisions of the Polish king. The new constitution was not only sanctioned, but also created by his magnificent, eminent mind, which constitutes a new lesson for the world."

Obviously, King Stanisław August Poniatowski could have done little for Poland if it had not been for the fact that at the highest positions of the legislative power there were people enlightened enough to rise above their own particular as well as group interests. They had already signalled their presence during the so-called Partition Parliament (1773–1775). At that time, however, they were too weak to successfully oppose the external and internal forces which threw the country into anarchy and weakened its position in Europe. They became stronger during the Four-Year Parliament (1788–1792), also known as the Great Parliament. The international situation was to their advantage, in particular the conflict between the coalition of the so-called southern (Spain, France, Austria and Russia) and northern countries (England, Holland, Prussia and Sweden). Already during the first phase of the Great Parliament these people managed to make Stanisław Małachowski (1736–1809) the Marshal of the Parliament. Although previously opposing the king's projects, he was a politician who in the crucial moments of the Parliament was the pillar of the king's party and the co-author of the project of the constitution. He was supported by the group called "Kuźnica Kołłątajowska" [Kołłątaj's Forge] (their leader was Hugo Kołłątaj). The passing of the constitution (in 1791) met with positive reactions not only from a part of Polish society, but also abroad. The French press wrote that "Poland is in the grip of the same fire of freedom as France and this fire will spread from the Vistula to the west towards the Rhine and to the North."[2]

In this "fire of freedom" mentioned by the French press, one can obviously see the influence of the French – especially of Montesquieu's *The Spirit of the Laws* and *The Declaration of the Rights of Man and the Citizen* from 1789. But what can also be found are attempts to rise above the vested interests of particular groups and the commencement of thinking not about one's own privileges but about a man and a citizen who remains a man and a citizen also

[2] Cf. ibidem, p. 231 ff.

when he or she does not possess any Church or noble titles. It was supposed to encompass everyone – also those who by the grace of God and historical coincidence were on the king's throne. Perhaps even Louis XVI, the king of France at that time, realized this, but he would not agree to such equality with common citizens. Ultimately, this led him to the gallows. King Stanisław August, on the other hand, behaved like an enlightened monarch should have behaved in such a situation – that is, he fraternized with the People. This was also noticed and appreciated by outside observers of the Polish political scene.[3]

Obviously, there is no liberalism without freedom, but it is also not possible in practice without wisdom, responsibility, far-sightedness, great decision-making skills and acting in such a way that the greatest number of people possible feels attracted to its major ideas. Liberals were not the only ones to point this out. However, in contrast to others, they connected these virtues not only with the conduct of particular people, but also with the activities of such a numerous collection of communities which constitute a nation. This is why education was so important in their social programmes. The precursors of liberalism in Poland can be accused of many faults, but not the fault of overlooking the significance of education for broadening and strengthening the sphere of civil liberties. One of these precursors of modern education was the above-mentioned Hugo Kołłątaj (1750–1812), the reformer of elementary and secondary education (including his original Cracow Academy). Liberalism is also impossible in practice without frugality, especially the frugality of the socially important groups, such as, for example, the middle classes. Kołłątaj writes about this in his writings, for example in *Listy skierowane do Stanisława Małachowskiego* [Letters Addressed to Stanisław Małachowski]. Here, in a surprisingly apt way, he points out both the main political dangers facing the Commonwealth of Both Nations and the main causes of its economic decline. He also presents a remedial programme which in actual fact gave his country a good chance for a better future.

Elements of this programme already appeared in his early speech to the members of the Commission of National Education (in 1776).[4] Here, he

---

[3] The American "Gazette of the United States" on August 5th, 1791 wrote that on May 3rd "the patriotic King Stanisław August [...] adamantly refused to be accompanied by anyone from his usual guard, but he mixed with senators and common citizens and was frequently lost from view in the crowd." In a September issue it was added that he was "the king of wonderful Mind and Principles, the king of Wisdom and Virtue," "wise because of experience, prudent because of examples, enlightened by philosophers..." (ibidem, p. 234 ff.). This opinion could be considered a hint as to how all holding the highest offices in the country should act – not only in the times of Stanisław August.

[4] Cf. H. Kołłątaj, "Stan oświecenia w Polsce w ostatnich latach panowania Augusta III (1750–1764)" [The State of the Enlightenment in Poland in the Last Years of August III's Rule

draws attention to the interdependence between democracy and education ("in a despotic country the act of perfect education cannot be even undertaken"), freedom and education ("the act of education should be worked on in a free nation") and freedom, wisdom, work and the right civil attitude ("in such a short time your wisdom and work in the shape of a communal medicine will transform the nature of the whole civic body: it will root out musty prejudices, introduce everywhere the good practice of civic skills, restore the need for conversation and a harmony of hearts which is craved for and necessary for the delight of a free country"). Kołłątaj finishes his speech with revolutionary accents. He talks about "introducing national education to village huts as well as to palaces." Whereas Kołłątaj did not claim that the success of this undertaking rested on removing from those palaces all those who were either uneducated or unwilling to learn, it was nonetheless clear to anyone familiar with the reality of the Jacobin France. Such pronouncements resulted in naming Kołłątaj as the "Polish Robespierre" in the last phase of the Four-Year Parliament.

During this period he wrote a few political treatises. Among the more important ones is *Anonima listów kilka* [Several Letters from an Anonymous Writer]. In the part entitled "O poprawie Rzeczpospolitej" [On Improving the Polish Republic] he writes – referring to physiocratic theories – about the need to base the Polish economy on agriculture ("I consider the earth to be the only treasure and a man's hand the key without which these treasures cannot be attained") and to link agricultural production with the taxation system ("the capitation tax is the most natural, in accord with the lawful gratitude of every man which he is obliged to manifest towards his Motherland for its care and protection"), and also to make this system transparent, clear and impenetrable ("tax should be collected in such a way that masses of treasure cannot be hidden away"). In his letters, he not only refers to physiocratic conceptions, but also to other economists, including the ideas of Adam Smith. Similarly to the author of *An Inquiry into the Nature and Causes of the Wealth of Nations*, Kołłątaj perceives the sources of the wealth in craftsmanship, trade and exchange; he asks, "Where could one find such a profit?" and answers: "In the cities which by the state authority were given so much aid and support that they can call themselves flourishing and wealthy. [...] What was, for example, Kalisz in the times of Zygmunt III, where 300 clothiers could have settled accounts? The persecution of religious dissidents brought downfall to Kalisz and populated Wroclaw [...]. The trade oppressed at one wall will look for freedom at another; cities fall where duty is raised; they lift themselves where trade finds its com-

(1750–1764)], in idem, *Wybór pism naukowych* [Selected Research Papers], Warsaw 1953, p. 77 ff.

fort. Poznan rose on the downfall of Torun..." These statements contain the germ of the free market concept. What follows are propositions that can be treated as liberal ideology. Kołłątaj writes that "common freedom will make us independent and thus truly happy." He expresses similar thoughts in other works from the time of the Four-Year Parliament. For instance, in *Uwagi nad pismem Seweryna Rzewuskiego* [Remarks on the Pamphlet by Seweryn Rzewuski], he claims that after dethroning Louis XVI, the French "restored human rights, became a free people and crushed the despotic power of ministers."

During the last years of his life, Kołłątaj wrote one of his more significant philosophical treatises entitled *Porządek fizyczno-moralny, czyli nauka o należytościach i powinnościach człowieka wydobytych z praw wiecznych, nieodmiennych i koniecznych przyrodzenia* [The Physical-Moral Order, or the Science of the Entitlements and Obligations of Man Arising From the Eternal, Invariable and Necessary Natural Laws, 1810]. He writes that "man is subject to natural laws which are common to all other beings; he also has, however, special, self-contained laws that make him different from other beings." They are "moral laws, which nature has made man subject to almost the same extent as to physical laws. [...] Among moral laws one of the utmost importance is that every man is born with special obligations, specific only to himself, to which are bound obligations, that is conditions, as it were, under which he is to use his entitlements."[5]

These "entitlements" are – in today's terminology – the "rights" which were so strongly demanded before the outbreak of the Great French Revolution, and later written on revolutionary banners and defended on barricades. In the French *Declaration of the Rights of Man and the Citizen*, from 1789, the top position belongs to the right to freedom, then comes (in article II) the right to "possession, security and resistance to oppression." These rights appear in a different order in the *Declaration* of Jacobins from 1793. There, the first is equality, next (also in article II) "freedom, security and possession." While writing his treatise, Kołłątaj gave up his earlier Jacobinism and moved towards a more moderate republicanism.

His treatise centres on an attempt to convince the reader that there can be no "entitlements" without the fulfilment of obligations and that it is a consequence of the "physical-moral order." Kołłątaj writes that "the rights, or natural acts operate in us, in spite of us, or, to put it more clearly, without the effort of our will: they are inborn skills, strengths and rules which cannot be isolated and distanced from us without destroying our mechanism in part or in its totality. Entitlements are like benefits which nature has conferred upon

[5] Cf. H. Kołłątaj, *Porządek fizyczno-moralny...* [The Physical-Moral Order...], in idem, *Wybór pism naukowych* [Selected Scientific Papers], op. cit., p. 253 ff.

us through its eternal and invariable laws [...]; obligations are duties necessary to be fulfilled, if we are willing to keep them, for us to be sure of our entitlements." After substantiating their close interrelationship (which in its entirety relies on the traits ascribed to human nature), Kołłątaj goes on to present these "entitlements" and obligations. He begins with freedom, but not freedom understood either as the right to "possess things, goods, offices, titles which do not serve others," or as "being free from the duties which others are bound by," but "the freedom of a man considered with regard to his needs, energies, entitlements, obligations and relations with other things." This is already clearly stated in the title of chapter IX, which is devoted to this issue, and in the opening sentences. In the later part of the work, he discusses the difference between freedom and lawlessness as well as the connection between freedom and reason, good manners, social feedback and their various limitations.

Kołłątaj deals similarly with the "natural equality among people," discussed in chapter XI. First, he firmly rejects its understanding as an equality of everyone in all respects ("in some respects people are equal, in some they are not"), then he presents a resolute *votum separatum* for the conviction that savages were equal and they lost their equality after they moved from living in reclusion to living in society. Next, he tries to demonstrate that it is not natural equalities, but inequalities which form the basis of social relations ("the father is his children's natural superior, in the household there is a host, in the nation there is one who is given the protective power"), and finally he asserts that the only option is "equality in relation to rights," by which he understands that "all offices, titles and magistrates do not introduce any inequality. They are established for everyone to equally make use of the benefits of one's own rights as well as obligations."

The treatise ends with a comparison of man's "entitlements" and obligations. It contains nothing that cannot be found in *The Declaration of the Rights of Man and the Citizen* from 1789. It is of course written in Polish and in a way which is approachable for the mind of an enlightened Polish reader. For example: in the discussion of the first "entitlement" it is said that "a human being belongs to himself only; he is his only owner by the gift of nature, which is the Highest Cause, to which he is exclusively responsible." While discussing the first obligation, it is claimed that, among other things, "a man should preserve his individuality as a whole, i.e. keep it alive and healthy [...], defend it against assaults," etc.

Stanisław Staszic (1755–1826) also made his mark in the liberal tradition in Poland. He was one of the more philosophical minds among the representatives of the Polish Enlightenment. First he studied in Poznan (he graduated from the seminary and in 1779 received holy orders), and then at universities in Leipzig, Göttingen and Paris (he studied physics and history in the Collège de France). His stay in France was particularly important in shaping his views. There, he met one of the then most distinguished naturalists L. Buffon (Staszic later translated his *Epochs of Nature* into Polish) and conducted geological research in the Alps. In 1781 he returned to Poland and became the tutor of chancellor Andrzej Zamoyski's sons.

In the years 1784–1788 he wrote *Uwagi nad życiem Jana Zamoyskiego* [Remarks Upon the Life of Jan Zamoyski] dedicated to the "knight's estate" but in fact addressed to the whole nation. Already at the beginning he presents the dramatic situation of the country divided among great powers, "under the slavish yoke of the Prussian," resembling the besieged Carthage and at the same time devoured by inner conflicts. "Great nation! How long are you going to remain in this heartlessness? Do you want to perish and leave nothing but infamy?"[6] These exclamations and questions were accompanied by the description of the problems which had to be resolved by the Polish Republic so that it could be saved from annihilation. The first of these problems was public education. According to Staszic, it is the only way to shape "peaceful and good citizens." A case in point for him is the Academy founded by Jan Zamoyski. It is, however, an example of wasted rather than exploited opportunities, because this university, at first with a good education programme, quite quickly became similar to the Church universities and instead of educating "enlightened and peaceful citizens" it transformed into "a school of blind, quarrelsome people, weak at heart and body" (actually, it was closed in 1784). The main instigator of this downfall is the theology in which "blind faith leads to perfection" and its closest ally is "systematic [i.e. a scholastic] spirit;" this was the reason why "for two thousand years people have not been able to think." In France, which was waging war against the Church, such pronouncements were nothing surprising. But in a country so strongly attached to the Church as Poland, they caused quite a stir and made many readers of *Uwagi* feel outrage.[7]

In his treatise, Staszic not only demonstrated his anticlericalism, but also presented solutions which in his view could remedy poor education. The first step was to reformulate its mission. Staszic claims that it should make "the man and citizen truly happy." "Since this happiness of the man and citizen is inseparable from the whole society, because the happiness of society results from the usefulness of all

[6] Cf. S. Staszic, *Uwagi nad życiem Jana Zamoyskiego* [Remarks Upon the Life of Jan Zamoyski], in idem, *Pisma filozoficzne i społeczne* [Philosophical and Social Writings], vol. 1, Warsaw 1954, p. 9 ff.

[7] The radical nature of opinions contained in Staszic's treatise led to publishing the first edition (1787) anonymously, with Heilsberg as the publication place (in fact, it was printed in Zamosc).

its inhabitants, therefore the aim of state education should be the usefulness of the citizen." In order to realize this mission, an appropriate education programme was deemed necessary. Staszic suggested such a programme. Its most important element was moral teaching: "This teaching should most frequently and clearly inculcate in the young that a man owes everything to himself and no one else owes anything to him; that surrendering to another person a part of what he owes to himself is necessary to create the obligations of mutual participation; that he alone should take care of his proper possessions; that man's first duty is to work; that in every class of society idleness makes a man harmful towards himself and others." Next comes a "national" teaching ("moral teaching instantly requires domestic geography, writings on the nation's history, the natural history of one's own district, arithmetic, and geometry combined with experimentation") and then "the history of neighbouring countries, national laws, rhetoric and treasury studies."

He considers these subjects as basic and obligatory. Others depended on the type of school and the level of education (for instance, in vocational schools, students should be taught "handicraft and craftsmanship"). The higher level contains such subjects as "astronomy, natural history, chemistry, physics and medical education." The last was to be taught at "the main school," that is, at university, and in the process "teachers should provide as little theory as possible so that proper experiments can be the teaching method." Of course, such a programme requires adequate teachers, funds, management, etc. Staszic does not neglect these issues either and notes the Commission of National Education as one of the praiseworthy institutions.

A similar structure is evident in the remaining part of *Uwagi* On the one hand, Staszic severely criticizes the present state of affairs and, on the other, provides concrete suggestions for resolving the problems. For example: the part entitled "Prawodawstwo" [Legislation] contains criticism of "the estate of nobility" ("with minds debased by luxury, effeminate and prone to slavery") and its rights (including *liberum veto*). The part entitled "Władza wykonawcza" [The Executive Power] berates absolutist monarchism and praises "ancillary" monarchism ("to become the king is to become the first civil servant and the first servitor of the whole nation"). The part entitled "Władza sądownicza" [The Judiciary Power] decries the whole judiciary system in Poland as well as the rights and practices exercised by given types of courts ("the sluggishness in judging is the great flaw of our tribunals"). Finally, the part entitled "Wolne obieranie królów" [The Free Royal Elections] criticizes the Polish electoral system, etc. In total, there are a dozen such parts, and the last one (the nineteenth) contains not only an appeal to Poles to save their country from the ultimate annihilation, but also a warning that "they will lose freedom unless they sacrifice class liberties."

The continuation of *Uwagi* is Staszic's *Przestrogi dla Polski* [Warnings for Poland], a treatise dating back to 1790 and also published anonymously. It opens with "Przemowa imieniem narodu polskiego" [Oration on Behalf of the Polish Nation] and the appeal to "magnates and nobility" to admit that they "do not constitute all Polish people, but merely a part" and most of all they should strive to be useful to the nation. Thus, if need be, they ought to defend it with a sabre and – as the estate which "has absolute power in Poland" – they should pass just and useful laws for the nation ("there should be such laws that the nation's conscientiousness, population and wealth grows continually"). The preface ends with an appeal to the nobility to pass the constitution – not a partial or "patched up" one, but "an entirely new constitution, encompassing the entire Polish nation."

This appeal introduces, as it were, an examination of conscience for the nobility. In the next dozen chapters, Staszic enumerates their "cardinal sins," such as upholding the rules and privileges which are against nature or violating basic human rights; "Equality, freedom and possession are the most necessary and the most basic consequences of human rights. No one is born with the privilege of idleness and wealth or is destined to work and remain in poverty. [...] No one is born with the stamp of servitude, dishonesty, scorn and shame of a life taken from them, and no one is born with the privilege of nobleness, power, respect and honour. Only usefulness provides equality among people."[8] This part ends with the admonition addressed to "lords, or magnates" that "theirs will be the most severe fate if Poland disintegrates."

The next chapters present analyses of the situation of various social groups either those comprising the Polish nation or those living in Poland. In the first place, Staszic presents those who "nourish the Polish nation," i.e. farmers. There are relatively few farmers on the gigantic territory of Poland, which resembles a wild forest. "If you are lost and you find a village, you have to find a man there. He was raised by violence, he is afraid of everything, he hides from another man as if from an enemy in his cave with no windows or chimney. Cities in such a country are not much different from villages, perhaps only by the greater stench of more numerous Jewish rogues who, as more knowledgeable, [...] poison and suck from the poor farmer the last drop of blood, not yet wrung out from him by work." These anti-Semitic statements also appear in the latter parts of *Przestrogi*.

[8] Cf. S. Staszic, *Przestrogi dla Polski z teraźniejszych politycznych Europy związków i z praw natury wypadające* [Warnings for Poland Resulting From the Contemporary Political Relations in Europe and Laws of Nature], in idem, *Pisma filozoficzne i społeczne* [Philosophical and Social Writings], vol. I, op. cit., p. 187 ff.

Apart from criticizing the nobility and Jewish community, Staszic was no less strict towards the clergy. The fact that he himself was a clergyman did not stop him from openly asserting that the clergy "misbehaves," runs "schemes for the country's ruin" and its elite, that is, "the richer bishops" and are distinguished by "ugly greed." He suggests that Church possessions be taken by the Treasury ("not only the possessions of bishops, but of all Polish clergy") and transformed into an "eternal lease" (in this way, the Polish Republic was to gain money for the army). He also advises the Parliament to forbid the so-called "composites" (obligatory payments made by parishioners for the rectory). Additionally, he proposes: firstly, to radically reduce Church offices ("apart from the rector and bishop, all the clergymen are unnecessary, because they are harmful, as they use other people's work to feed themselves"); secondly, to transform common clergymen into common civil servants ("the rector is a national civil servant"); thirdly, to do away with useless priories and Church offices. All this is not only permeated with the spirit of French Jacobinism, but also French Bonapartism.

Neither the writings of Kołłątaj and Staszic nor the political activities of other Polish patriots managed to prevent Poland from losing independence for over one hundred years. It was partitioned among three of the then superpowers: Russia, Prussia and Austria. This led to, among other things, stunting the development of Polish liberal thought for many years, and to such an extent that historians can barely find its traces in Poland.[9] The weakness of the Polish liberal tradition is pointed out by Jerzy Szacki in his monograph *Liberalizm po komunizmie* [Liberalism after Communism]. In the introduction he writes about "the lack of liberal tradition in East European societies" and about "the manifest inconsistency between liberalism as a theory and practice of civic society, formed in the capitalist West, and the reality of backward East European societies with their semi-feudal socio-economic structure, sparse and weak middle class and the dominance of an illiterate peasant population who in the times of B. Constant and J. S. Mill were serfs and to a large extent remained within the boundaries of a barter economy."[10] Szacki also indicates such non-economic reasons for the weakness of liberalism in Poland – the

[9] Barbara and Marek Sobolewski write that "to the east of Germany the influence of liberal thought becomes gradually weaker" and "the fate of liberal thought in Poland can be considered quite typical of many East European countries." Cf. B. and M. Sobolewski, *Pojęcia i ewolucja liberalizmu* [The Concepts and Evolution of Liberalism], in B. Sobolewska, M. Sobolewski (eds.), *Myśl polityczna XIX i XX w. Liberalizm* [Political Thought of 19th and 20th Century Liberalism], Warsaw 1978, p. 72 ff.

[10] Cf. J. Szacki, *Liberalizm po komunizmie* [Liberalism after Communism], Cracow 1994, p. 62 ff.

"long years of 'the Golden Liberty of nobles' which first led to Poland losing independence and then to popularizing independence slogans in society." What is more, "in Poland, an important non-economic factor hindering the reception of liberalism was undoubtedly Catholicism, which played a significant role in public life. [...] Similarly to other East European countries, all this made liberalism in the 19th century as well as later in Poland an unpopular way of thinking."[11]

[11] Ibidem, p. 65 ff.

Part II

Contemporary issues

Chapter 5

Liberal ideology

The variety and diversity of liberal ideas, postulates and suggestions for solving fundamental social problems frequently makes it difficult to indicate where liberal ideology begins and ends. As a result, liberal ideology is often treated as a kind of "sack" for throwing in and taking out various ideas.[1] I am of the conviction that despite the significant diversity of liberalism, its ideology is no such "sack." What is more, I believe that it is possible to establish a list of this ideology's leading ideas, postulates and propositions. However, such a list must remain open, that is, one can add new entries to it or cross out those which are justifiable in some circumstances. This is the first of the proposed ways to define liberal ideology. The second one, complementary to the first, concerns indicating those ideologies with which liberalism did not find common ground when achieving its social objectives. It must be emphasized at this point that liberal ideology – like any other ideology – cannot be reduced to a simple juxtaposition or enumeration of those ideas, postulates and propositions. This is because they have undergone significant changes over a period of many years.

One of the works which clearly present this issue is Pierre Manent's *An Intellectual History of Liberalism*. The starting point for him is Niccolò Machiavelli's (1469–1527) concept of "the creative power of evil" and the points of arrival are the ideas of Alexis de Tocqueville (1805–1859), such as the concept of modern democracy which, according to the author of *On Democ-*

---

[1] Ideology is understood here – to a large extent in accordance with Karl Mannheim – as a collection of general ideas, postulates and social propositions which in many respects complement each other, express diverse needs of various social groups and justify the necessity of undertaking actions which could lead to the satisfaction of those needs. Cf. K. Mannheim, *Ideology and Utopia. An Introduction to the Sociology of Knowledge*, London 1954.

racy in America, contains in itself ideas concerning the equality of conditions, representative society, assemblies and the new despotism. Between these two time frames, separated by several hundred years, Manent places Thomas Hobbes (1588–1679) with his concept of a Leviathan (an Absolute Sovereign, for whom the fundamental reason for its existence and operation is "the right of the individual"), John Locke's idea of limiting the power of this and all other Leviathans as well as his idea of work (it is supposed to make man the owner of the things he creates), Charles Montesquieu's (1689–1755) idea of the division of power, Benjamin Constant's (1767–1830) idea of constructive opposition (its actions are to ensure the sovereignty of the people) and his idea of the eloquent orator (who can pave the way for liberalism thanks to the power of his sharp "criticism and irony"), and François Guizot (1787–1874), who promoted the idea of liberal government and was a liberal Prime Minister in France.

In the introduction to his book, Manent claims that "one of the principal 'ideas' of liberalism is [...] that of the 'individual.' The individual is that being who, because he is human, is naturally entitled to 'rights' that can be enumerated, rights that are attributed to him independently of his function or place in society and that make him the equal of any other man."[2] Today they are called human rights and it is generally considered obvious that men are entitled to them. However, when liberal ideology was in the process of being born at the end of the 18th century as well as in its later and more mature stages of development, many issues concerning those rights were debatable.

This becomes clearly noticeable when one juxtaposes the two French *Declarations of Man and the Citizen* from the period of the Great Revolution. The one from 1789 propagates an undoubtedly narrower understanding of equality. It is assumed in its pages that individuals who can and do have the right to use the rights they are entitled to are at least enlightened enough to, for instance, be able to elect their own government (art. III), act in a way that does not harm other men (art. IV), do only the things allowed by law (art. V), cooperate in person or through their representatives in the process of creating the law (art. VI), etc. All the remaining eleven articles also require intellectual enlightenment.

The *Declaration* from 1793 propagates a wider understanding of equality, because it does not require of all citizens to possess an enlightened mind to such an extent. Already in its preamble the notion of the *people* is employed and the assumption is that it is enough for the legislators in the first place, and, to some extent, civil servants secondly to be enlightened. The *people* are expected to be enlightened only to such a degree that the functioning of the representative system is made possible. When it turned out that this kind of solution opens the door for social terror (which was confirmed by the Jacobin

[2] P. Manent, *An Intellectual History of Liberalism*, Princeton, New Jersey 1995, p. xvi.

rule in France), liberals started to emphasize the *equality of a reasonable minimum.* Explaining how this term is to be understood, Guizot states that "all careers should be open everywhere, free competition enabled everywhere and authorities united with a higher necessity;" and nothing more. Clearly, this narrowing of the idea of equality resulted in narrowing the notion of the *people* and the *nation.* Guizot applies this term to "lawyers, notaries, capitalists, workshop owners and merchants;" and no one else. Although in the second half of the 19th century there were once again attempts to advocate a wider understanding of the formula of equality, none of the more reasonably thinking liberals supported the equality of every individual in all respects.

Out of the above and similar internal differences within liberalism there emerged its two historical wings, that is, the right one, called *aristocratic liberalism,* and the left one, called *democratic liberalism* or – in short – *demoliberalism.* A wide retrospection of their thought can be found, for example, in a collection of selected writings by leading liberals entitled *Myśl polityczna XIX i XX wieku. Liberalizm* [The Political Thought of the 19th and 20th Centuries. Liberalism]. From the point of view of the authors of this collection, the main ideas of liberalism are:

a) the idea of the historical progress of mankind ("Liberals are optimistic in this respect, they believe not only in the possibility of improving the people and conditions in which they live, but in the real improvement taking place in the course of history");

b) granting "the individual primacy over society" ("liberalism is an individualistic ideology");

c) the idea of "freedom above all else" ("the liberals' preference for freedom must be treated as a logical consequence of the first fundamental assumptions");

d) treating private property as a kind of sanctity ("Considering private property as the basis for free society has been and is still presently one of the basic constituents of the liberal credo");

e) the idea of the limited role of the state in social life ("The postulate to limit the function of the state is again a logical consequence of liberals' attitude towards property");

f) and, closely connected with the above, the idea of the separation of powers. ("The classical division of power into legislative, executive and judiciary does not exhaust the full extent of this rule from the viewpoint of the liberal doctrine. It could take various forms, but it has always been connected with the mistrust of sovereign, or unlimited, power.")[3]

---

[3] B. and M. Sobolewski, "Pojęcia i ewolucja liberalizmu" [The Concepts and Evolution of Liberalism], in B. Sobolewska, M. Sobolewski (eds.), *Myśl polityczna XIX i XX w. Liberalizm* [Political Thought of 19th and 20th Century. Liberalism], Warsaw 1978, p. 9 ff.

These ideas have been considered the lowest common denominator for the entire liberalism of the 19th and 20th centuries, whereas their detailed clarifications and direct supplements form the basis of the division into right and left-wing liberalism.

In contemporary literature, the former is called *moderate liberalism* while the latter *radical liberalism*. It is difficult, however, to establish a clear borderline between the two. Therefore, it should only be noted that in the past the former was recognized by its supporters, who opted for a governing system in the form of a constitutional monarchy, while the advocates of the latter were in favour of a republic. From the viewpoint of liberalism as a whole, their standpoints also differed in such fundamental issues as:

a) the understanding of social freedom. All liberals would not agree with the statement that freedom in a civilized society is about allowing the citizen to do what he wants (because it would inevitably lead to social anarchy), but even when they agreed that the citizen can do everything that does not harm other human beings, moderate liberals added to this a long list of freedom's limitations, whereas the list by radical liberals was considerably shorter;

b) the understanding of social equality. In general, all liberals agreed on the above-mentioned *equality of a reasonable minimum* and the need to take into account "the social benefit" while determining this minimum, but moderate liberals were in no doubt that there have to be limits and barriers for social careers and free competition has to operate within certain restrictions;

c) the understanding of the relations between the basic rights and obligations of citizens. They agreed with respect to the basic rights and that in a civilized society there has to be a connection between the range of these rights and the accomplishing of civic obligations, as these, in turn, are connected with social benefits. Moderate liberals, however, tried to defend at least some of the rights of those people and institutions whose fulfilling of obligations and usefulness was seriously questioned from the beginning of the 18th century (this concerned not only people with aristocratic titles but also the clergy and the Church), while radical liberals did not understand the reasons for defending this *ancien régime* and wanted the same law for everyone and the same evaluation of the realization of civic obligations, which in practice meant the frequent emergence of new social elites;

d) the understanding of the relations between the government and the governed. They agreed that it is natural and necessary that society is divided into those who govern and those who are governed and that the former have to have the consent of the latter, but those who govern also have to act for the common good and not only for personal gain as well as be subject to social control. The two wings differed, however, with respect to who should and who should not be given the elective franchise and the right to stand for election.

In general, the discussions on the above issues continued throughout the entire 19th and 20th centuries. At the beginning they concerned, among other things, the problem of property requirements and education. As a rule, moderate liberals set quite high electoral standards, while radical liberals generally opted for setting those standards relatively low, believing both in the natural reasonableness of the average man and in the natural mechanism which makes it possible for the true social elites to emerge from the masses.

1. Liberalism and conservatism

No in-depth analyses of the relationships between liberalism and conservatism are necessary to conclude that they have always taken opposite sides. On various occasions, both groups supply the arguments in favour of this view by bandying slogans: anticonservative ones in the case of liberals and antiliberal in the case of conservatives. However, it also has to be underlined that these oppositions took various forms in the past and have taken various forms till the present. Actually, it has not always been the case that liberals have not been able to reach an agreement with conservatives on any socially important matter or to contract temporary alliances for the sake of such matters. Of course, this has always been easier for moderate liberals and conservatives rather than for those located at the extremities. Nonetheless, there have been cases in which a left-wing liberal went hand in hand with a right-wing conservative. Obviously, sometimes it looked and sounded odd not only for the politicians from other parties, but also for outside observers of the political scene. And it has always been a serious problem for liberals and conservatives as well, because it has posed a threat to their social credibility and could make one confused by their frequently convoluted arguments "for" and "against." Therefore, it seems worthwhile to attempt answering the question what conservatism was before, and is now.

The etymology of the term conservative is quite easy to explain. It is derived from the Latin word *conservatus*, which means "the preservation of something." Its equivalents in modern languages are, for instance, *conserver* in French and *conservation* in English. It is much more difficult, however, to define conservative ideology or at least to point to such ideas, postulates and social propositions with which every conservative would always agree. This is confirmed by, for example, an attempt to define conservatism undertaken by Karl Mannheim, who was after all a specialist in various social ideologies.

This attempt is carried out in the treatise entitled *Myśl konserwatywna* [Conservative Thought]. Mannheim, however, does not start with an ideology but with a reflection on the style of thinking and next (after the presentation of a few general remarks on the relationships between those styles and their social background) he moves on to a concrete example. This concerns the German conservatism of the first half of the 19th century. It is analyzed by comparing it to the social background of various narrative styles and various social ideologies in countries like France and England.

The results of this analysis show that whereas in the past conservatism was actually one of the main opponents of liberalism, there was neither a single conservatism nor a single liberalism and, in fact, those which were present in the above-mentioned countries formed significantly different and, historically, changing narrative styles and ideologies. These differences resulted from, among others, social differences in those countries and a varied distribution of political forces. For instance: "[...] the relationships between the Tories and Whigs in England until 1790 are almost impossible to describe in German terms. This is particularly connected with the fact that the party called 'liberal' in Germany bore no resemblance to English Whigs at all."[4] A similar case concerned liberalism and conservatism in France.

According to Mannheim, the discrepancies between the two reached "the most abstract forms" but did not go – similarly to England – "beyond convoluted and complex stages." In Germany, these discrepancies attained "the highest level of logical and structural cohesion," which makes it possible to "grasp very clearly the influence of social forces on the logical structure of thinking." For Mannheim, this fact justifies the choice of conservative ideology existing in the first half of the 19th century in German countries as the relatively best historical basis for the enumeration of typically conservative ideas, postulates and social propositions.

In the second part of his treatise entitled *Sens konserwatyzmu* [The Meaning of Conservatism], Mannheim attempts to articulate these ideas, postulates and propositions. In the first place, he draws attention to traditionalism, which is the historical predecessor of conservative ideology and is defined as "the tendency to stick to old models, vegetative ways of living considered common and universal." In the light of these explanations, conservatism is traditionalism's "child" but a relatively late one, because it is "born" only in modern

[4] "The fact that basic intentions and practical social motives behind conservatism manifested themselves in such a distinct and clear form in German thought seems to spring from the almost ancient structure of German political life, rendering a situation in which even a partial intermingling of parties and social classes – which was a fact in England – impossible. Even more important was the ability of German conservatism to defend property at the times of danger and the fact that while conservatism for quite a long time developed rather independently from liberalism, the latter allowed conservatist elements to penetrate their grounds." Cf. K. Mannheim, *Myśl konserwatywna* [Conservative Thought], Warsaw 1986, p. 13 ff.

times, growing up in the 18th and 19th centuries and reaching maturity not until contemporary times. Thus, when answering the question about the differences between conservatism and traditionalism, Mannheim concludes that "people experience and behave in a conservative way (in contrast to the traditional way) so far and only so far as they join one of the development phases of this objective thought structure (usually the contemporary phase) and behave in accordance with this structure or simply reproduce it in its entirety or in part, or through developing it through its adjustment to specific circumstances."[5]

Next, Mannheim outlines "the social background of contemporary conservatism" (obviously, it varies in different countries), "the morphology of conservative thought," including its "basic intention" (it is the same as in traditionalism, the difference being the emergence of a conservative awareness of "sticking to old models") and "the theoretical core of conservative thought" ("the crucial problem for conservatives was the opposition to thinking which centred around that of the natural law").

These concise characteristics already contain comparisons of particular elements of conservative and liberal thought, including such fundamental issues as the understanding of freedom and equality. "Revolutionary liberalism (connected by Mannheim with English and French thought – my comment) understood freedom as an economic phenomenon consisting in freeing the individual from medieval dependence on the state and guilds. In terms of politics, freedom was understood as the right of the individual to act according to their own will, and especially as the right to make full use of inalienable human rights. According to this concept, the individual encounters restrictions only when he invades his fellow men's freedom. Thus, equality is a logical supplement for this kind of freedom."

Such an understanding of freedom and equality posed a special challenge and task for conservatives. They made attempts at solving it by proposing for example "their own idea of freedom which differed from the liberal one."[6] For Mannheim, such attempts were made by German thinkers such as Adam Muller (d. 1829), Friedrich Julius Stahl (d. 1861) or Karl Friedrich von Savigny (d. 1861). Although Mannheim in his treatise also refers to the attempts undertaken by French and English conservatives, their names appear only occasionally and in general these references are not accompanied by any detailed analyses of the suggested solutions. This is unfortunate because this would

5 Ibidem, p. 37 ff.

6 "[...] they developed a concept which might be called a qualitative idea of freedom as distinct from the revolutionary-egalitarian concept. Counterrevolutionary opposition instinctively understood that the idea of freedom as such should not be attacked, so they focused on a more deeply hidden idea of equality." Ibidem, p. 48 ff.

actually reveal the complexity of the relationships between various strands of European liberalism and conservatism.

Now, let me add a few words about French conservatism.[7] Its progenitor is considered to have been Jacques Benigne Bossuet (1627–1704), the author of, among other things, *History of the Variations of the Protestant Churches* [Histoire des variations des Églises protestantes, 1688]. Here, he developed and tried to justify a thesis that these Churches cannot be recognised as authentic since they are changeable, internally diverse and they keep differentiating into smaller congregations. He also considered different varieties of the then existing mysticism as an inauthentic form of religiosity which indeed called into question the meaning of the existing and visible Church (its representative mystics believed that they possessed a special gift for establishing direct contact with God). His polemic with François Fénelon (1651–1715), the author of *The Adventures of Telemachus, Son of Ulysses* [Les Aventures de Télémaque], who presents the institution of monarchical authority in an ambiguous light, became famous. For several years, Bossuet was the tutor of the successor to the crown and remained an apologist for Louis IX's style of monarchical authority. Louis IX was an absolute monarch who liked to emphasise that his power came directly from God and, therefore, he was solely responsible to God for the way he exercised his power.

Bossuet adopted the same attitude in his *Politique tirée de l'Écriture sainte* [Politics Drawn from the Very Words of Holy Scripture]. This apology for France's absolute monarch and French Catholicism led him to publish, in 1682, *The Declaration of the Gallican Clergy* – a paper recognised as the ideological credo of Gallicanism. In the light of this credo, the French king is to be independent (in secular matters) of the Pope, while the French bishops are to be the direct inheritors of the Apostles, and as such they should remain equal to the Bishop of Rome.

French conservatives who were active at the end of the 18th century and in the first decades of the 19th century followed this line of thought concerning secular and religious powers, which they claimed society was obliged to obey. The new indicator of their ideology became apparent in their attitude towards the French Revolution of 1789.[8] All of them evaluated it critically,

[7] This could also apply to British or Italian conservatism. Each of these countries had their own liberal as well as conservative traditions and, which is equally important, these developed in their internal (including domestic) and external oppositions. The same issue is raised by K. Mannheim. In his footnote 86, he mentions this problem as the "Anglomania of the young Adam Muller," who "abandoned his friendly attitude towards England after British foreign policy had been changed").

[8] "Its assessment is the starting point for all the systems of counter-revolutionary thought, even those which, apparently, were just a repetition of the ideas and concepts known for ages." Cf. J. Szacki, *Kontrrewolucyjne paradoksy. Wizje świata francuskich antagonistów Wielkiej*

applying epithets to it such as: "the height of absurdity and moral decay," "the explosion of sinful pride," or simply "an act of bandits." Representatives of extreme conservatism (referred to in literature as *ultras*) claimed that the revolution had failed to bring any positive solutions or to introduce any new social order. According to one of them, Louis de Bonald (1754–1840), "the revolutionary legislators granted rights to disorder only to consolidate it." On the other hand, the representatives of moderate conservatism, such as for example François-René de Chateaubriand (1768–1848), claimed that revolutionary changes had brought something positive, like the fact that they had managed to awaken the Christian conscience from lethargy.[9]

Nowhere are the differences between ultra- and moderate conservatives as visible as in their axiology, especially if applied to the scale of values they followed. The former usually used a two-value scale which sharply presented their alternative "either – or." The latter, though they did not completely surrender the two-value scale, also referred to a wide range of indirect values which were relative but, at the same time, meaningful enough to enable humankind to "march" towards a universal harmony which would constitute the ultimate destination of the history of mankind. What this march was like in the past is described by F.-R. de Chateaubriand in his *Génie du christianisme* [Genius of Christianity, 1802].

Pierre Ballanche (1776–1847), on the other hand, described in his *Essay on Social Institutions* [Essai sur les institutions sociales] what this march might look like in the future. What is characteristic is that Ballanche did not perceive Napoleon Bonaparte (unlike ultra-conservatives) as some sort of devil incarnate but as "the strongest personality that has ever dwelt on earth since ancient times, a personality whose intelligence has achieved the highest level of development," but also one with whom the development of "moral feelings" could not keep pace.

At the turn of the 19th century, however, it was not the moderates but the ultra-conservatives that were at the forefront of conservatism, with Joseph de Maistre (1754–1821) as their most prominent figure. It seems that already his biography turned him into an ultra-conservative. He was a high-ranking official in the court of the king of Sardinia. He lost his position when the Kingdom of Sardinia was annexed by France in 1792. In 1803, his own monarch sent him on a diplomatic mission to St. Petersburg, where he stayed for 14 years, in vain exerting himself to gain for the king of Sardinia the Tsar's favour. Dur-

Rewolucji 1789–1815 [Counterrevolutionary Paradoxes. The French Antagonists of the Great 1789–1815 Revolution and Their Visions of the World], Warsaw 1965, p. 34 ff.

[9] Cf. R. Chateaubriand, *De la Monarchie selon la charte* [The Monarchy According to the Charter], Paris 1816, p. 4 ff.

ing his stay in Russia, Maistre wrote *The St. Petersburg Dialogues.*[10] His book is one long indictment of the French Revolution, of the French revolutionaries and their allies, as well as of all the worst that had happened in France and its dependent territories.

When writing about the French Revolution of 1789, de Maistre described it chiefly as having been "inherently wrong." For him, revolutionaries were mere puppets of the powers over which they could not keep any control ("the more thoroughly we research into the seemingly most active personages of the Revolution, the more clearly we begin to notice something passive and mechanical in them"). As for their allies, he depicted them as not only insane but also as the ones who infected others with their insanity. Among this group of the condemned one may find both Protestants (who "in a frenzied way tried to replace books with authority, and authority with the offices of preacher") as well as philosophers of the Enlightenment whom he characterised as "loathsome individuals" whose writings "made people lazy" and who were "infatuated with disputes, persisting in their views and despising the views of others."[11]

The ideological premises that provide a basis for this severe criticism of the Enlightenment philosophers are definitely theistic in character. According to Maistre, everything that is, everything that really exists, is directly or indirectly God's work. What is more, he was convinced that this work was created for man and for man's sake. If, therefore, man is a social being, he is one not because of any inner need or because of any sheer coincidence, but by God's will and in accordance with God's plans, whose implementation is the primary goal of the history of mankind. The Creator is to implement His plans through such wholes which exist in the form of particular countries and through such parts which are formed by particular individuals: "each nation, like every individual, has been appointed a certain mission which they ought to accomplish" – each has been given a suitable mission and each has been equipped with appropriate means to carry it out. The conclusion that follows is that particular nations are, and must be, different in terms of language, spirit, customs, political regimes, etc. Another conclusion is that the political forms of government suitable for one nation do not necessarily have to be suitable for another ("despotism is for one nation as natural and legitimate as democracy for another"). Maistre claims that the Creator, through these nationality differences and diversities, leads humankind to unity, and He leads people towards global unity through

[10] Cf. J. de Maistre, *Les Soirées de Saint-Pétersbourg ou Entretiens sur le gouvernement temporel de la Providence*, Paris 1821.

[11] He described these philosophers as "fanatical people. They are proud of their knowledge but they have no idea about anything..." Cf. J. de Maistre, *Des Constitutions politiques et des autres institutions humaines*, Strasbourg 1959, p. 81 ff.

particular nations' achievements by partial unities, such as moral or political unity. The influence of human activity in achieving these unities is to be minimal. Maistre adamantly opposed the Enlightenment concepts of a social agreement which assumes that creationism is not divine but human. He used to call such a social agreement a *chimera*.

In light of the above views, the French Revolution of 1789 appears to have been an inevitable historical catastrophe. It was inevitable because a great part of this one-of-the-most Christian nations in Europe tried to replace God's law with human rights, the system of Divine Governorship with human governorship, and "common reason with human reason reduced to individual possibilities."[12] In Maistre's view, this catastrophe happened with God's knowledge and by God's will. Its aim was to convert humankind to the path of humility, submission to God's will, and piety.

In this context, the social postulates which de Maistre put forward seem to sound quite natural. These can be summed up in the following appeal: "to combat, to destroy, to limit and to tighten." This means: combating various novelty seekers, especially philosophers, who treat the Teaching of the Church with utter contempt; destroying various "sophisms" like "the sophism of universal freedom and equality;" the limiting of the access of lower social classes to education and to public offices; and tightening of censorship and police control over society. Views like these match the apology of the Spanish Inquisition. Such a vision also corresponds with his apology of the Executioner (in *The St. Petersburg Dialogues* he stated that "all discipline rests on the Executioner: he is a real scourge and bonds the human community").

2. Liberalism and socialism

The relationships between liberalism and socialism were no less complicated and – using K. Mannheim's expression – "entangled" in various social backgrounds, as was the case of the relationships between liberalism and conservatism. In certain respects, however, they were antagonistic in character. This antagonism gained momentum especially in times and in places in which liberals and socialists competed for acceptance and social support, and such moments and places proved plentiful.

It is worth recalling here that the concept of *socialism* itself was used for the first time in 1834 in the writings of Pierre Leroux (a Saint-Simonist) referring to those who "criticise and condemn individualism." Although they not always put an equals sign between different forms of individualism and

[12] Cf. J. de Maistre, *Considérations sur la France. Oeuvres Complets*, vol. I, Paris 1940.

different varieties of liberalism, they still classified liberals into the group of those who practised and approved of individualism. Socialists believed that liberal concepts, postulates and social slogans were the driving force behind the sort of capitalism in which a man of hard labour did not count. The one who counted was the capitalist who wanted and was able to make such huge profits and raise such capital that would enable him to increase it. For this type of capitalist, it would certainly be most suitable if they were given freedom of action and if neither the state nor any other power having at its disposal an arsenal of means to efficiently influence social life interfered with their business.

Therefore, many a socialist was inclined to put equals signs between, for example, liberalism and the principle of free competition in the economy and between the ideology of liberalism and the ideology of *laissez faire*, even though their general principles and concepts are convergent in certain respects only.[13] These and other similar simplifications contributed to the fact that the history of the relationship between liberalism and socialism has been marked, to a great extent, by various polemics and differences in their views on the solution of basic social problems. Obviously, these differences varied from country to country.

In Germany, among the most controversial issues, and the one that caused the most passionate polemics, was the way the term *state* was interpreted. This issue was raised for the first time by the liberal Lorenz von Stein (1815–1890) in his *Socialism and Communism in Contemporary France* (1848). He wrote it in defence of liberal sanctities such as the individual's right to freedom, to private property and to a participation in power. He also made an attempt to show who and what could pose a threat to those rights. Among them was socialist ideology, which promoted the concept of the state as an institution standing above those rights, an institution which could both ration and temporarily suspend them.[14] It follows from this ideology that it is not the state that serves its individuals but that individuals serve their state. This antisocialist statement contains one more important theme of the state – class division. Stein had strong feelings against such a state, since he believed that it was not a state of law but a state of lawlessness or, which is the same thing, not a state of civil liberties but a state of enslavement of one part of the society by another.

[13] The author of the flagship slogan of laissez faire, i.e. *laissez faire, laissez passer – let us do as we will, let us move as we will*, is a French physiocrat Jean Vincent de Gornay. What he, and other physiocrats, meant was that there should be freedom of action in the economy, in which agriculture would form the basis for expertly developed economic management supported by the state. Only later did this recommendation become a kind of flagship for the supporters of capitalistic free-market economy.

[14] Cf. L. von Stein, *Socialismus und Communismus des heutigen Frankkreichs*, Leipzig 1848, p. 33 ff.

Friedrich Naumann's views were another important voice concerning this particular issue. Naumann (1860–1919) was the then renowned liberal publicist, the founder of "Die Hilfe" and a politician (in 1907–1910 he was a Reichstag deputy). In his speeches, he took into account the criticism of liberalism articulated from the point of view of socialism. In fact, he admitted self-critically that "former French and English liberalism kept plunging into the thought of freedom of the individual. This is and was its Alpha and Omega, and from this point of view, he questioned every thought of the socialist social system. [...] This old liberalism protested, with natural necessity, against state interference and against state industry. Did it not fight like a lion for the state to give its individuals freedom so that, without hindrance, they could move their hands and use their brains in the way they liked? This great faith in the individual, which used to be his sole object of interest, is now a living fire burning in the original liberalism, and it is this faith which hides a significant part of the eternal truth because in fact there is no progress without creative individual personalities. And if nowadays the main political question is whether this old idea of personality ought to be replaced by despotic socialism, all liberals ought to arise as one man [...] in order to call out: a creative individual is the primary element in the state and in national economy!"[15] The above statement exceptionally appropriately conveys both the ideological *credo* of the liberals' faith in the creative individual and their lack of faith in the state that was supposed to replace everybody and everything. Such an understanding of the state can be found, which not only F. Naumann but also other liberals claimed, at the root of socialist ideology.

Principal polemics between liberals and socialists also took place in Italy. Eminent political ideologists were frequently involved, such as, for example, Benedetto Croce (1866–1952) – on the side of the liberals – and Antonio Gramsci (1891–1937) – on the socialist side. Croce was a leading activist of the Italian Liberal Party, when between 1944 and 1947 he was the Party leader, while Gramsci was a leading activist of the Italian Socialist Party.[16] Both of them managed to combine their temperaments of activist and politician with the temperaments of a political publicist, ideologist and philosopher.

The former presented his antisocialist attitude most distinctly in his *Moral Aspects of Political Life*. On the one hand, he tried to describe the philosophical premises of liberal ideology and, on the other, to show how in essence it differed from socialist ideology. He claimed that liberal ideology was, beyond everything else, an attempt to "search for an optimal state," which meant

[15] Cf. F. Naumann, *Das Prinzip des Liberalismus*, in idem, *Die Politik der Gegenwart*, Berlin 1905.

[16] In 1921 it was transformed into the Italian Communist Party.

neither a theocratic nor an autocratic state but a pluralistic one, meaning one which left its citizens much room for activity "so that they could compete with each other and confront their powers, cooperate in harmonious disagreement," etc. He perceived and presented different varieties of socialist ideology as those being burdened with a double sin, meaning "the sin of theocracy and the sin of autocracy." Their visions of the future contained "the concept of a perfect kingdom, with no conflicts and composed of human beings equal before God." In their visions of the present, however, there appeared the concept of "the dictatorship of the proletariat," where this dictatorship was, like any other type of dictatorship, nothing but autocracy. That is why "socialism meets with the hostility of liberalism, which leads to conflicts between them [...]. For other reasons, meaning its specific demands, the conflict of principles would not have arisen because liberalism has no reason to oppose the increasing humanisation and the increase in the importance of the working class and agricultural workers. In its own way it strives to achieve this goal but it lacks the links of complete solidarity with capitalism and economic liberalism or with the economic system of free competition, and it can successfully allow different ways of establishing property and the production of goods..."[17]

Obviously, these conciliatory words could not satisfy the socialists as they did not express consent for socialist solutions; neither did they close the list of his accusations against socialist ideology. The list enumerated such serious accusations as the ones which claimed that socialism "professed equality understood in an external and mechanical way" (it was to be the basis for the so-called people's democracy) or that it wrote emotional and biased histories of humankind ("histories written by all sorts of reactionaries, clericalists, feudal lords, Jacobites, socialists and nationalists are always extremely emotional and biased, immature and pessimistic...").

Antonio Gramsci responded to such serious accusations in his, among other works, *Benedetto Croce's Historical Materialism and Philosophy*. His first line of defence for socialist ideology caused him to "bury himself" in the materialistic positions (a materialistic way of comprehending human history, basing the driving force on a socio-economic basis, relying on practice as the decisive factor of last resort, etc). His second line of defence was to strike his opponent with accusations that were usually used by the classics of Marxism, meaning Karl Marx and Friedrich Engels. The catalogue of these accusations is long. One of them accused Croce of mechanism ("the philosophical error of this philosophy lies in the fact that in the dialectic process, it is mechanically assumed that the thesis has to be preserved by the antithesis"), another

[17] B. Croce, *Aspetti morali della vita politica*, Napoli 1927; reprint: *Elementi di politica*, Bari 1966.

of speculativism ("his philosophy remains a speculative philosophy, which means that it is marked not only by a trace of transcendence and theology but by transcendence and theology themselves except that it has been liberated from the vulgar shell of mythology"). Gramsci also accused his opponent of idealistic historicism ("Croce's idealistic historicism is still in the theological-speculative phase"), and of amicability. ("Although Croce does not seem to be inclined to make intellectual concessions for the sake of religion," his attitude is "far from being militant.")[18]

---

[18] Cf. A. Gramsci, *Il materialismo storico e la filosofia di Benedetto Croce*, Torino 1948.

Chapter 6

Liberalism vs. totalitarianism

An important part in the liberals' fight for various social freedoms was their opposition against several forms of totalitarianism. In England, this first appeared as opposition against Catholic totalitarianism, also called Papism; however, when presented with the opportunity to be free of totalitarianism, it appeared again under the guise of their native Anglican Church, which endeavoured to take the place of its predecessor. Likewise in France, objections first emerged against the omnipotence of Rome, such as in Pierre Pithou's 1594 publication *Liberties of the Gallican Church*, among others. Only later was there opposition regarding the omnipotence of its absolute monarchs. There was a similar situation in the German Lands, except that the adversaries of totalitarian religion maintained peace for an extended period of time through a compromise which could be characterized by the phrase "whose realm, his religion." In Italy, the conflict with Rome did not take place as much under the pretext of attaining freedom from Catholic totalitarianism as it did for the purpose of achieving freedom from those rulers who, in the name of protecting their own interests, first came to an agreement with their enemies beyond the Alps, namely, the Spanish, French, and Germans, and second, enslaved their faithful. In some of these countries, liberals dealt with feudal totalitarianism earlier, while in others it was handled at a later time. Nevertheless, it can generally be said that by the end of the 18th and beginning of the 19th centuries, the conflict regarding totalitarianism had, for the most part, been settled.

At that time, totalitarianism had emerged with certain new elements, but was still significantly rooted in tradition. The result was the formation of socialism. This traditionalism was especially evident in the views of the then utopian socialists. Amongst them was Charles Fourier (1772–1837), author of *The Theory of the Four Movements* (1808). The central theme of this work can be summarized by the phrase, "minimum individualism yields maximum collectivism." Individualism was associated with anarchism, while collectivism to the predominance of harmony and social order. Directly following this line of thought is the realization that the less freedom of choice in society and the more planned, organized acts by superiors, the greater the fulfilment of life's necessities for all. In Fourier's opinion, however, the greatest planner of all was and would continue to be God. Concretely laying out the specifics, he described a vision of social life in which people live in relatively small communities of 1600 to 2000 people, called phalanxes by his own definition. These communities were meant to function as nothing less than a well-oiled machine, with every action being productive. This productivity was to be ensured by the work requirement imposed on each individual member of the phalanx, with children being required to take up work responsibilities at the age of three. An essential component in the life of the community was education, which should be universal and continue for nearly an entire lifetime, as well as the development of feasibly permanent and lasting interpersonal relationships, which would be furthered by maintaining residence in one large home called a phalanstère.[1]

These and other similar visions of social life, described by such utopists as Claude Henri Saint-Simon and Étienne Cabet, among others, were met with criticism from dissidents, including liberals. One of these critics was Émile Faguet. In the treatise titled *Liberalism*, he described socialism as an entity similar to monarchy and aristocracy, in that "they are the enemies of freedom."[2] According to Faguet, "socialism is merely a mutation of monarchism" because of its aspiration that "everything be executed by the state so everything could be controlled by the state, so that beyond the state nothing would exist."[3] If socialism differs from monarchism, they differ only in that in one country a monarch rules with his closest accomplices, while in another country, officials maintain command at various tiers of power.

1. Isaiah Berlin

In every case, the seriousness of the perceived threats to liberalism depended on the exact circumstances and experiences of those who posed the threats. Such attitudes towards these perceived threats were no different with regards to Isaiah Berlin (1909–1997). Berlin, of Russian and Jewish background, had

---

1 G. S. Jones, I. Patterson (eds.), *Fourier: The Theory of the Four Movements*, Cambridge 1996.

2 Cf. É. Faguet, *Le Libéralisme*, Paris 1902.

3 Ibidem, p. 265 ff.

lived in Latvia, but then later immigrated to England with his family in 1920. In 1935, he graduated from the prestigious University of Oxford, where he was later a professor for many years. His literary works were comprised of academic as well as popular scientific writings.[4] Two general problems are discussed in his works: Marxism and liberalism. He addressed the former and the latter as ideologies encompassing a rather rich philosophical basis with societal relevance. He himself was drawn to liberal ideas, but also found some truth in Marxist ones, especially in Karl Marx's own work. He stated that even if the ideas were unconvincing, they at least had historically justified views.

According to Berlin, Marxism and liberalism have certain elements in common, such as rebellion "against tyrants, priests, and militant philistines" and the "disinterested eloquence" of leaders of the incapacitated, who "are lifted by the common mood and for a moment speak not for their own class or milieu alone, but in the name of all the oppressed."[5] From the initial moment of the opponents' emergence, several differences also became evident between them. They differed in that "liberals believed in the unlimited power of education and the power of rational morality to overcome economic misery and inequality. Socialists, on the contrary, believed that without radical alterations in the distribution and control of economic resources no amount of change of heart or mind on the part of individuals could be adequate; or, for that matter, occur at all." Moreover, socialists, like conservatives, "believed in the power and influence of institutions and regarded them as a necessary safeguard against the chaos, injustice, and cruelty caused by uncontrolled individualism; anarchists, radicals, and liberals looked upon institutions as such with suspicion as being obstructive to the realization of that free (and, in the view of most such thinkers, rational) society..."

The paths of these two ideologies ultimately parted in 1903. At that time, there was a congress of the Russian Social Democratic Party. "During the discussion of what seemed at first a purely technical question – how far, centralization and hierarchical discipline should govern the behaviour of the Party – a delegate named Posadovsky inquired whether the emphasis laid by the 'hard' Socialists – Lenin and his friends – upon the need for the exercise of absolute authority by the revolutionary nucleus of the Party might not prove incompatible with those fundamental liberties to whose realization Socialism, no less than liberalism, was officially dedicated. He asked whether the basic,

[4] His most important writings are: *Karl Marx: His Life and Environment* (1939), *Historical Inevitability* (1955), *The Age of Enlightenment* (1956), *Russian Thinkers* (1978) and *Against the Current* (1979).

[5] See I. Berlin, *Political Ideas in the Twentieth Century*, in idem, *Four Essays on Liberty*, London 1969, p. 11.

minimum civil liberties [...] should not be infringed and even violated if the party leaders so decided." The response of Plekhanov, one of the creators of Russian Marxism, was: "Certainly, if the revolution demanded it, everything – democracy, liberty; the rights of the individual – must be sacrificed to it." Admittedly, Plechanow himself, an individual brought up in a tolerant and liberal tradition, had, unlike Lenin, later abandoned this position. Lenin went even further, since he demanded unlimited power for a small group of professional revolutionaries. He had an opinion regarding this, which affirmed that "it was useless to talk and reason with persons precluded by class interest from understanding and acting upon the truths of Marxism, but that the mass of the proletarians themselves were too benighted to grasp the role which history had called on them to play."

Berlin criticized communist totalitarianism but paid little attention to precisely how it abused power, or to its "crimes, terror, and repression," as stated in the words of the authors of *The Black Book of Communism*.[6] What he was interested in, however, was its intellectual history and the ideas of its founders. Berlin recognized Lenin as one of them, but not Karl Marx, who in his opinion, was a "typical nineteenth century social theorist, in the same sense as Mill or Comte," and who brought to light many real problems which he thought he had resolved. "He supported his solutions with arguments which he certainly supposed to conform to the best scientific and philosophical canons of his time."[7] According to Berlin, many different allegations could be held against Marx, but not any related to "the practice of Communist States and, more logically, of Fascist States." This nullifies any accusation that "he did not form critical minds or develop the ability to solve problems, nor the capacity for insight or intuition, which were presumed to bring about truth."[8]

---

[6] Cf. S. Courtois et al., *The Black Book of Communism: Crimes, Terror, Repression. Collective Works*, Cambridge – London 1999.

[7] "Whether his outlook was in fact as scientific as he claimed, or his solutions are plausible, is another question. What matters is that he recognised the genuineness of the questions he was attempting to answer and offered a theory with a claim to being scientific in the accepted sense of the term; and thereby poured much light (and some darkness) on many vexed problems, and led to much fruitful (and sterile) revaluation and reinterpretation." I. Berlin, *Political Ideas in the Twentieth Century*, op.cit., p. 24.

[8] "It consists in something which any nineteenth-century thinker with respect for the sciences would have regarded with genuine horror – the training of individuals incapable of being troubled by questions which, when raised and discussed, endanger the stability of the system; the building and elaboration of a strong framework of institutions, 'myths,' habits of life and thought intended to preserve it from sudden shocks or slow decay. This is the intellectual outlook which attends the rise of totalitarian ideologies [...], the state of mind in which troublesome questions appear as a form of mental perturbation, noxious to the mental health of individuals and, when too widely discussed, to the health of societies. This is an

These and other similar opinions show that the negative image of communism as a totalitarian social formation is contrasted with the rather positive image of Marx as presented by Berlin. To him, the Soviet Union under Stalin's rule was an example of the distortion of everything that was either a foundation or social consequence of this totalitarianism. Included among such dictates are the complete "subordination to the central plan, and the elimination of disturbing forces, whether by education or repression, has been enacted with that capacity for believing in the literal inspiration of ideologies [...] to which Russian thinkers of all schools seem singularly addicted. The Soviet pattern is clear, simple and deduced from 'scientifically demonstrated' premises."

Communist totalitarianism, similar to its fascist counterpart, was in Berlin's opinion the denial of those values which all liberals fought for, presently fight for and will assuredly continue to fight for. The major goal of their fight is most certainly freedom, but as history shows, freedom can be understood differently and implemented differently in the practise of social life. After all, freedom had already been discussed in ancient Greece. Berlin uses examples of such ancient thinker's statements, which he found praised freedom. Among the examples are quotes in the work of Herodotus, "the celebrated paean to liberty in the Funeral Oration of Pericles, as well as the speech of Nikias before the final battle with the Syracusans [...]." They and those Grecians who thought similarly about social life fought for freedom, which was understood to be a state in which citizens "are not slaves of any master, that they perform their civic duties out of love for their polis, without needing to be coerced, and not under the goads and whips of savage laws or taskmasters." Freedom was understood differently by Epicureans, Cynics, and Cyrenaics. For them, freedom meant "the complete withdrawal from public life" and consequently leading their own "life in their own world." Both understandings prove that "the issue of individual freedom, of the frontiers beyond which public authority, whether lay or ecclesiastical, should not normally be allowed to step, had not clearly emerged at this stage; the central value attached to it may, perhaps [...], be the late product of a capitalist civilisation, an element in a network of values that includes such notions as personal rights, civil liberties, the sanctity of the individual personality, the importance of privacy, personal relations and the like."[9]

In *Two Concepts of Liberty*, Berlin proposes differentiating between negative and positive freedom. The former of the two is related to the answer to the question: "What is the area within which the subject – a person or group of

attitude, far removed from Marx or Freud, which looks on all inner conflict as an evil, or at best as a form of futile self-frustration..." Ibidem, pp. 24–25.

[9] I. Berlin, *Introduction*, in *Four Essays on Liberty*, op. cit., p. xli.

persons – is or should be left to do or be what he is able to do or be, without interference by other persons?" However, the latter ties in with the answer to the question: "What, or who, is the source of control or interference that can determine someone to do, or be, this rather than that?"[10] To briefly summarize, the first kind of freedom is "freedom from..." (generally, from different forms of societal coercion), while the second is "freedom to..." (generally, to be "the master of your own fate"). The first of the two was addressed by "such libertarians as Locke and Mill in England, and Constant and Tocqueville in France." The second was discussed by those thinkers who believed in the liberating power of critical reasoning. In the opinion of Berlin, both Hegel and Marx were counted among them. Hegel thought the restraint of the people was the result of misunderstanding the specificities of public institutions and civic rights which sanctioned their existence, civic rights being "rights which can be rationally understood since they themselves are the result of reasoning." Marx went further, as he "offered social and economic hypotheses to account for the inevitability of such misunderstanding, in particular of the illusion that such man-made arrangements were independent forces, as inescapable as the laws of nature. As instances of such pseudo-objective forces, he pointed to the laws of supply and demand, or the institution of property, or the eternal division of society into rich and poor, or owners and workers, as so many unaltering human categories."

According to those philosophers and others similar to them, "I am free if, and only if, I plan my life in accordance with my own will; plans entail rules; a rule does not oppress me or enslave me if I impose it on myself consciously, or accept it freely, having understood it, whether it was invented by me or by others, provided that it is rational, that is to say, conforms to the necessities of things." Berlin emphasized that freedom, which ultimately shows itself to be an understanding of what is necessary, is "at the heart of many of the nationalist, Communist, authoritarian, and totalitarian creeds of our day." He also calls attention to the fact that it is relatively easy to turn away from the philosophy of the "Objective Reason" and "teleological determinism of Hegelians" to a "more voluntaristic philosophy," or also completely abandon the concept of reason and consider oneself an "inspired artist, who moulds men into patterns in the light of his unique vision."[11]According to him, the explanation provides a sufficient argument to side with negative freedom.

---

[10] I. Berlin, *Two Concepts of Liberty*, in *Four Essays on Liberty*, op. cit., pp. 121–122.

[11] For such an "artist" mankind is "the raw material upon which I impose my creative will; even though men suffer and die in the process, they are lifted by it to a height to which they could never have risen without my coercive – but creative – violation of their lives [...].

This support of negative freedom was the cause of much debate. The author of *Two Concepts of Liberty* called it an "open and fruitful discussion." Some of his opponents accused him of "invalidating determinism," while others stated that he confused it with fatalism. To the first, he responded that his position does not mean supporting voluntarism, but rather "self-determinism" or "weak determinism," meaning the kind in which determination relates not to the behaviour of people but to their characteristics; nevertheless, people are capable of changing those characteristics. To the second group, among them Ernest Nagel, he admitted that there was a fundamental difference between determinism and fatalism, but he considered this accusation to be the result of the misunderstanding of his ideas. The defence of negative liberty signifies only that, regarding the individual, it is considered that "other people do not interfere in what that individual desires to do," and regarding their relationship with others, that he or she is free "from chains, from imprisonment, from enslavement by others." There is yet another essential addition: "Least of all does it call for abdication by individuals or groups from democratic self-government of the society, after their own nicely calculated corner has been made secure and fenced in against others, leaving all the rest to the play of power politics."[12]

2. Karl Raimund Popper

Karl Raimund Popper (1902–1994), like Berlin, belonged to those European intellectuals who, in fear of fascism, left their country and sought protection abroad. He was born in Vienna, finished his university degree there, and later began lecturing at that university. He ultimately attained his doctorate in the field of psychology. He was equally interested in philosophy, particularly cognitive matters. In 1936, he took leave to travel to England for a study visit and was later employed at Canterbury University College where he worked until 1945. In 1946, he took up residence in England where he began working at the London School of Economics. In 1964, in recognition of his academic accomplishments, he was knighted. Especially notable are his achievements in the field of the philosophy of science.[13]

The appearance of communist and fascist threats to Western civilization compelled him to more carefully examine the different forms of totalitarian-

---

Every dictator, inquisitor and bully who seeks some moral, or even aesthetic, justification for his conduct." Cf. ibidem, pp. 150–151.

[12] Cf. I. Berlin, *Introduction*, op. cit., p. lxi.

[13] *The Logic of Scientific Discovery* (1934) belongs among his most important works from that period.

ism. The result of this was, among other works, the discourse titled *The Open Society and Its Enemies* (1945). In this work, he argues not with the implementers of totalitarian ideologies as much as with the founders of the ideology, by whose ideas they were able to lure in the masses. In the introduction to the first edition of his work, he wrote that the motive that guided him was the "conviction that, if our civilization is to survive, we must break with the habit of deference to great men [...] [for] some of the greatest leaders of the past supported the perennial attack on freedom and reason." Nevertheless, in the preface of his second edition published in 1950, he added that "Seen in the darkness of the world situation of 1950, the criticism of Marxism which it attempts is liable to stand out as the main point of the book."[14]

The work does in fact have two main antagonists, with Karl Marx being mentioned here along with Plato, who must be specially examined "with highly critical eyes," having played a role, perhaps not so much a small role as an important one in advancing the ideal of a closed society. It was Hegel who Popper acknowledged as the philosopher who "not only developed the historical and totalitarian theory of nationalism, he also clearly foresaw the psychological possibilities of nationalism."

Everything, nonetheless, started with Plato. None of his predecessors believed to the same extent as this author of the works *Statesman*, *The Republic* and *Laws* that "the law of historical destiny, the law of decay, can be broken by the moral will of man, supported by the power of human reason."[15] This is the framework of what is called social engineering. "The social engineer does not ask any questions about historical tendencies or the destiny of man. He believes that man is the master of his own destiny and that, in accordance with our aims, we can influence or change the history of man just as we have changed the face of the earth." He is considered a dissenter of historians. He remains convinced that "intelligent political action is possible only if the future course of history is first determined." In Plato's works, both beliefs are simultaneously present, resulting in a combination typical for "quite a number of social and political philosophers." Popper also adds the historical premises and religious connections concerning the emergence of this particular dichotomy, one of which is the attempt "to escape the Heraclitean flux, manifested in social revolution and historical decay." "It may contribute to the understand-

[14] Cf. K.R. Popper, *Open Society and Its Enemies*, Princeton 1950, p. v ff.

[15] "Plato believed that the law of degeneration involved moral degeneration. Political degeneration at any rate depends in his view mainly upon moral degeneration (and lack of knowledge); and moral degeneration, in its turn, is due mainly to racial degeneration. This is the way in which the general cosmic law of decay manifests itself in the field of human affairs." Ibidem, p. 23.

ing of Plato's theory of Forms or Ideas if we compare it with certain Greek religious beliefs." He also points out its specific sociologism, since "much of Plato's sociology is presented by him in such close connection with his ethical and political demands."

From this emerges Plato's vision of the ideal nation, meaning a nation divided into three classes, "the guardians, their armed auxiliaries or warriors, and the working class," but pragmatically into two classes composed of "the military caste – the armed and educated rulers – and the unarmed and uneducated ruled, the human sheep." Along with the category of citizens, the vision includes the category of slaves. In Popper's opinion, this is an expression of Plato's contempt for Athenian democracy. In this nation, all power is found in the hands of the ruling class, which is made possible thanks to communism and "the abolition of private property."[16] In order to maintain and reinforce this power, it is essential to educate and shape helpers, as well as to strengthen the belief that the ruling class is the superior race, since "the race of guardians must be kept pure." In this instance, it can be said that Plato's communism is based upon the same principles as its modern forms.

Popper not only pointed out these analogies but also tried to prove that concurrences appear in other important matters, such as in the attempt to give communism the status of historical necessity, presenting it as something "as inevitable as the rising of the sun, or the cycle of the seasons," adorning it in a scientific "costume," and presenting it as a programme of global justice. This last matter was addressed in full in the chapter VI of his discourse. The sixth chapter, titled *Totalitarian Justice*, lists the foundations of this justice. In the list, Popper included "the strict division of the classes," "the identification of the fate of the state with that of the ruling class," "the ruling classes' monopoly of things like military virtues and training," the "censorship of all intellectual activities of the ruling class, and a continual propaganda aiming at moulding and unifying their minds" and the self-sufficiency of the state as "it must aim at economic autarchy."

The intellectual link tying Plato's totalitarianism with its contemporary forms is Hegel's philosophical beliefs. This philosopher instilled modern totalitarians with the cult of the state, history, and nation, among other things. In the light of his *Elements of the Philosophy of Right*, a nation should be venerated "as the manifestation of the Divine on earth," and history should be recognized as our Judge, whose every judgement is fair. Moreover, its people

[16] "Since all property is common property, there must also be a common ownership of women and children. No member of the ruling class must be able to identify his children, or his parents. The family must be destroyed, or rather, extended to cover the whole warrior class. Family loyalties might otherwise become a possible source of disunion..." Ibidem, p. 49.

should be treated as a community imbibed with spirit, which functions and reveals itself throughout history. All of these elements converge in Hegel's admiration for the Prussian state ruled by Frederick William III, a state which was nearly classified as a classical example of a closed society. Hegel's idea was to later become a foundation of fascism, in which his racist ideology was incorporated. ("The formula for a fascist brew is the same in all countries: Hegel plus a dash of 19th century materialism."[17])

Popper recognized Marxism as "so far the purest, the most developed and the most dangerous form of historicism." As far as Karl Marx himself is concerned, he was characterized by certain outstanding intellectual advantages: "[...] his sense of facts, his distrust of verbiage, and especially of moralizing verbiage, made him one of the world's most influential fighters against hypocrisy and pharisaism. He had a burning desire to help the oppressed, and was fully conscious of the need for proving himself in deeds, and not only in words. His main talents being theoretical, he devoted immense labour to forging what he believed to be scientific weapons for the fight to improve the lot of the vast majority of men." He, however, appeared to be a false prophet given that "his prophecies did not come true" and, what is even worse, he was a destructive prophet, since "he is responsible for the devastating influence of the historical method of thought within the ranks of those who wish to advance the cause of the open society." This Marxist historicism manifested itself in his theory of class struggle. In light of this, "the history of all hitherto existing societies is a history of class struggle," as is equally shown in his theory of the state that "the state, in brief, is just part of the machinery by which the ruling class carries on its struggle." These and other various supplementary theories regarding changes occurring in economic systems, among others, were introduced by the creators of Marxism as the one fully scientific explanation for the prominent regularity of social life. In Popper's opinion, an additional crucial characteristic of Marxism is its desire to be more than just a historical prophecy or school of thought, as it also proposes a political programme. Popper rates this programme as "extremely poor" as "its poverty is a consequence of the third-rate place which it attributes to political power in the hierarchy of powers," but in spite of this, it became the inspiration for two "great Marxist Parties, the Communists and the Social Democrats. Both these parties were entirely unprepared for such a task as the transformation

[17] "[...] racialism substitutes something material for Hegel's 'Spirit,' the quasi-biological conception of Blood or Race. Instead of 'Spirit,' Blood is the self-developing essence. [...] The transubstantiation of Hegelianism into racialism or of Spirit into Blood does not greatly alter the main tendency of Hegelianism. It only gives it a tinge of biology and of modern evolutionism." K.R. Popper, *Open Society...*, op. cit., p. 256 ff.

of society. The Russian Communists, who found themselves first within reach of power, went ahead, entirely unaware of the grave problems and the immensity of the sacrifice as well as the suffering which lay ahead. The Social Democrats of Central Europe, whose chance came a little later, for many years shrank from the responsibilities which the Communists had so readily taken upon themselves. [...] One can say that the split between the Central European Communists and Social Democrats was one between those Marxists who had a kind of irrational faith in the final success of the Russian experiment, and those who were, more reasonably, sceptical of it."[18]

Popper was, to a lesser degree, interested in the political history of communism and more so in its intellectual history. It is comprised of these elements, the first being cultivated by vulgar Marxists of economic historicism ("the average Vulgar Marxist believes that Marxism lays bare the sinister secrets of social life by revealing the hidden motives of greed and lust for material gain which actuate the powers behind the scenes of history"). Next is Marx's prophecy, stating that "all classes except a small ruling bourgeoisie and a large exploited working class are bound to disappear, or to become insignificant." Finally there is the theory of "proletarian social revolution," where a violent civil war between the two classes remaining on the historical scene is assumed. A derivative of this is, among others, an anti-democratic platform, for the politics of "Marxist parties can be characterized as one which makes workers suspicious of democracy," and the fostering of internal and external enemies of open society, such as fascists.[19]

As for the question, "what is this open society, or what should it be?" Popper did not give a clear answer. It can be admittedly acknowledged that it is generally the opposition to a closed society, but this is a significant oversimplification of the problem. With the criticism of the second of the two societies emerge observations leaving no doubts that the first (open society) was not built in the past and is not being built presently through simple contrasts of the

[18] "When I say 'irrational' and 'more reasonably,' I judge them by their own standard, by Marxism; for according to Marxism, the proletarian revolution should have been the final outcome of industrialization, and not vice versa; and it should have come first in the highly industrialized countries, and only much later in Russia. This remark is not, however, intended as a defence of the Social Democratic leaders whose policy was fully determined by the Marxist prophecy, by their implicit belief that socialism must come." Ibidem, p. 333.

[19] In light of the communist thought: "Thus the destruction of democracy through the fascists could only promote the revolution by achieving the ultimate disillusionment of the workers in regard to democratic methods. With this, the radical wing of Marxism felt that it had discovered the 'essence' and the 'true historical role' of fascism. Fascism was, essentially, the last stand of the bourgeoisie. Accordingly, the Communists did not fight when the fascists seized power." Ibidem, pp. 352–353.

following types: exclusive and egalitarian, collective and individualistic, enslaved and free, totalitarian and democratic, or non-humanitarian and humanitarian. All of these must be taken into consideration, since without them the values cherished in open society become incomplete and unclear.

Popper calls his vision of society a humanitarian theory of justice. The first comments on this topic appear in the chapter devoted to the criticism of Plato's totalitarian justice; here he posits that, among others, "the humanitarian theory of justice makes three main demands or proposals, namely: (a) the equalitarian principle proper, i.e. the proposal to eliminate 'natural' privileges, (b) the general principle of individualism, and (c) the principle that it should be the task and the purpose of the state to protect the freedom of its citizens."[20] In later parts of these reflections he attempts to explain misunderstandings tied to the postulates, such as the equating of individualism and egoism, or freedom and lawlessness. In light of the criticism of Hegel's tribalism, a threat for egalitarianism, individualism, and citizens' freedom shows itself in the veneration of the state, history, and the nation (of Prussia, for example). On the other hand, regarding the criticism of Marx's economic historicism, a threat, among others, is the worship of production, namely, material goods, as well as the theory of class struggle.

Now concerning the general question addressed at the end of the work: "Does history have any meaning at all?" Popper admittedly replies contradictorily, that "history does not have meaning" whilst he simultaneously adds that "we can add meaning to it," neither by posing as prophets nor invoking any one of them, but rather by "learning to do things as well as we can, and looking out for our mistakes." These conclusions would arguably be endorsed by many different liberals today.

It should be, nevertheless, clearly stated that Popper's approach to liberalism is specific in more than one manner. This is reinforced by, among others, his critical reply on the topic of public opinion. The ideas were encountered in his report presented in 1954 in Venice to the members of the liberal Mont Pelerin Society. He considered this opinion to be a certain kind of myth, similar to the myth of the "average Joe," otherwise "a simple man" or "the masses." Not without sarcasm did he note that "the masses, fortunately, rarely speak with one voice, and different "average Joes" on different streets differed to the same degree as liberals gathered in a single conference hall." During this lecture he explained his understanding of the concept of *the liberal*. By a liberal he does not mean "a sympathizer with any one political party but simply a man who values individual freedom and who is alive to the dangers inherent in all forms of power and authority."[21] In this sense Popper is clearly a liberal.

---

[20] Ibidem, p. 94.

[21] K. R. Popper, *Conjectures and Refutations*, London 2002, p. xiii.

It is worth noting that, according to such an expert in and supporter of liberalism as John Gray, "despite its wide influence, the political thought of Karl R. Popper has received, until recently, remarkably little systematic attention from academic political theorists. Hailed by Isaiah Berlin as the most formidable of Marxism's living critics and reviled by Marxists as a prominent luminary of that White Emigration whose pernicious influence is mainly responsible for the ideological rejuvenation of a moribund reactionary culture, canonized as a prophet of freedom and enterprise and lumped together with such despised conservatives as Oakeshott, Namier and Butterfield as one of those who want only 'to keep that dear old T-model on the road by dint of a little piecemeal engineering, Popper incontestably has been a storm centre of several ideological controversies. [...] The form of critical rationalism which has been developed by some of its disciples has been seen, both by its proponents and by its enemies, as the foremost contribution to the contemporary struggle against irrationalism. Yet, though its central importance is attested by the long-standing controversies it has engendered and by its impact on a broad range of disciplines, Popper's work in social and political philosophy has not received anything like the sustained critical examination it warrants."[22]

3. Raymond Aron

Raymond Aron (1905–1983) was a philosopher and finished his study of philosophy in 1927 in the École normale supérieure, but his interests were much more diverse, as he discussed various contemporary social problems. Included in his rich academic repertoire are many discourses in the field of sociology and political science.[23] He was also an esteemed political publicist; for many years he wrote articles for "Le Figaro." He simultaneously took part in academic and journalistic activity and teaching in French institutes of higher education, including the École Nationale d'Administration and the Sorbonne.[24]

In the discourse *Democracy and Totalitarianism* [Démocratie et totalitarisme, 1965] he presented two constitutional models that he thought were typical of modern society, that is, constitutional-pluralist and totalitarian, based on the monopoly of power attained by one political party. In this discourse, he also

---

[22] J. Gray, *Liberalism. Essays in Political Philosophy*, New York 1989, p. 10 ff.

[23] R. Aron is the author of such works as: *Le grand schisme* (1948), *La société industrielle et la guerre* (1959), *Paix et guerre entre les nations* (1962), *Essai sur les libertés* (1965), *Les étapes de la pensée sociologique* (1967), *La revolutions introuvable* (1968), *De la condition historique du sociologue* (1971), *Histoire et dialectique de la violence* (1973), *Les dernières années du siècle* (1984).

[24] Some of his lectures were also printed. Among them are: *Eighteen Lectures on Industrial Society* [Dix-huit leçons sur la société industrielle, 1962] and *Class Conflict* [La Lutte de classes, 1964].

attempted to demonstrate circumstances causing the emergence of the latter form of the two types of power administration in several different countries, such as in fascist Germany, Italy, Spain, Portugal and communist Russia. In light of these analyses, every instance of totalitarianism had its foundation in anti-liberal and anti-democratic ideologies. A cause for such popularity in the West was the inefficiency of democratic structures, the corruption of authority, as well as the poverty of the hardest working individuals. In Russia, communists also executed their power to an unimaginable degree of terror, first in 1917–1921 regarding the opposition's groupings, later regarding "class enemies," or kulaks and other members of formerly privileged classes, and even later regarding also inconvenient members of their own party (their victims made up approximately 70% of central committee members of the Communist Party of the Soviet Union, as well as around 60% of all delegates at the 17th congress of the party), and finally regarding the entire society. Aron invoked the reminiscences of Nikita Khrushchev, both a first-hand witness and implementer of terror, that for Stalin an "enemy of the people" was anyone who disagreed with him in any regard.[25]

The analysis of the Soviet system, for Aron, was the basis for the differentiation between the five varying characteristics of totalitarianism. He included among them:

1. The monopoly of a single party on political activity;
2. The support of political activities by the ideology, which is to become the official truth of the state;
3. The power's accumulation of all that could be used for violence as well as the operative means of persuading society to their official truth such as radio, television or press;
4. The subordination of the vast majority of economic and professional activity to state control.

To briefly summarize, "from now on everything becomes state activity and every activity is subordinated to the ideology so that any mistake made in economic or professional activity is simultaneously an ideological mistake."[26]

Many comments on modern totalitarianism can be found in an interview conducted in 1981. It is titled: *Observer* and Participant [*Le spectateur engagé*, published in Polish as *Widz i uczestnik*] and includes a type of account of events in which he was a first-hand participant, or at the very least an attentive witness. His interviewers were Jean-Louis Missika, an economist, as well as Dominique Wolton, a sociologist.

---

[25] Cf. R. Aron, *Démocratie et totalitarisme*, Paris 1965, p. 278.

[26] Ibidem, p. 284 ff.

The beginning of his recollections falls on the years 1930–1933, that is, the period of time when he was first in Cologne, then in Berlin. The Germany of that time was ingrained in his memory as a country that opposed the provisions of the Treaty of Versailles, lived through an economic crisis, and tended more and more clearly towards anti-Semitic nationalism and fascism. The last of the three was hardly noticeable at that time, even for Aron, a Frenchman of Jewish background, who never revealed his "hereditary lineage." But all this changed after the Nazi's rise to power. The "time of suspicion" had then begun. Some were suspected of having Jewish lineage, others of being anti-Semitic, and yet others (e.g. French Jews) of "reacting so strongly to Hitlerism, given that they were more Jewish than French." For Aron himself, leaving Germany meant, among other things, the attainment of political maturity, principally comprising of an understanding of who Hitler was, what state socialism was, and what Nazi Germany's intentions were. Dominique Wolton brought to his attention the fact that in the years 1934–1938 he made no use of this knowledge, and further states that, first, he was not yet able to write in such a way as to appeal to the general public, second, he was little known as a philosopher, third, he had no means to enter into political activity, fourth, among the French elite "the philosophy of passivity" dominated at that time, and finally, Nazism did not yet exist in France.[27]

For the sake of clarity, it must be added that in those years he was neither a liberal nor a liberal sympathizer. At that time, he considered himself a left-ist, and even a supporter of the Popular Front. In the interview *The Committed Observer*, he admitted that he supported them until he discovered its "political economics," more specifically "the economics of those who ruled France at that time."[28] He described these individuals as "completely ignorant" and found their economics to be absurd. In this interview he also states that, like many other intellectuals, he then succumbed to the appealing ideas of Marx, and even posits to this day that "Marx's [form of] Marxism is extremely interesting." From this arises the question of his attitude toward "communism, or the Bolshevik Revolution and the Soviet experiment." Aron admits that he knew little about it at that time in spite of the fact that he had travelled to Moscow,

[27] It is worth citing this fragment as what Aron then acknowledged to be the justification for the "philosophy of passivity" regarding fascist threats. "It is obvious that I opposed fascism, however, at that time, it was my opinion that there was no fascism in France. Since the need at that moment was to keep the French unified, I believed that any move originated from a particular passion would weaken the state and thus expand the reach of the German threat." See R. Aron, *Widz i uczestnik* [Observer and Participant], Warsaw 1992, p. 44.

[28] This pertains to, among others, Leon Blum (1872–1950), leader of the Popular Front and Premier of the coalition government in the years 1936–1937.

but was nevertheless "partially neutral toward Marx, slightly interested but not fascinated, and especially disinclined toward violence since he had even then exhibited a liberal temperament."[29] It should be added that he was a liberal of the opinion that "the supporters of the USSR were significantly more amicable than others" but he despised "individuals with a pro-Hitler orientation;" "it required war and the post-war period for these strange ties to finally be broken." Aron generally remembers the years leading up to the outbreak of World War II as a time of many political misunderstandings, as well as erroneous appraisals which were difficult to explain. This especially applies to Nazism and Sovietism. It was his belief that neither Conservatives, Socialists nor intellectuals truly understood him, and in 1938 they were of the opinion that antagonizing Hitler "meant running the risk of war."[30]

He saw the outbreak of World War II as "mayhem conjured by one individual and not by a historical movement like communism." To him, this signified a draft (in a troop unit conducting meteorological forecasts). After France was defeated and Marshal Pétain gave his capitulation speech on March 22nd, 1940, Aron got across to England and joined the Gaullists. After a brief period of taking on the function of record keeper for a tank unit, he was offered a position in the editorial office of the newspaper "La France libre."[31] In spite of the fact that the newspaper was considered to be a Gaulistic organ, "representing free France," his relations with General de Gaulle were cold. The General did not like that in "La France libre," "analysis predominated over propaganda" and Aron "did not like the cult of personality surrounding the General." From the wider context of their statements, it can be concluded that above all, they differed in their attitudes towards the Vichy's administration. General de Gaulle naturally considered the administration to be comprised of traitors and collaborators, but for Aron, they wanted what the majority of French people wanted, meaning peace and calm, as well as reconciliation between de Gaulle and Pétain. After his interviewers brought to his attention the fact that it was also an administration that, on October 30th, 1940, issued an anti-Semitic law, he gave a rather surprising clarification regarding the fact that he remained silent about this matter as well as the general matter of

[29] "I did not believe in Messianism or millenarianism. For this reason, I was not thrilled with Bolshevism in the 1920s. In the 1930s, however, we were more and more overwhelmed by the obsession with totalitarianism. Totalitarianism being not only Hitler, but also Stalin." Ibidem, p. 49.

[30] Aron recalls his meeting that year with Jean-Paul Sartre and Simone de Beauvoir: "Both were enthusiasts of Munich and, as pacifists, they concluded that to use the lives of the people at one's disposal is beyond anyone's right." Cf. ibidem, p. 61.

[31] The articles published in it later appeared in the book under the befitting title *Widz i uczestnik* [Observer and Participant], op. cit.

the extermination of Jews in Europe. He stated he did not write about this "because he is a Jew," and beyond that, "the war was being fought to liberate France, it was being fought against totalitarianism, against despotism, and not for the Jews."[32]

The end of the War for France, among others, was a time of reparation after the occupation period, but amends were not made for France's actions towards the Jews. In Aron's opinion, "France declined the examination of its conscience." It was also a time of animated political and intellectual life as well as political re-evaluations with "neither the left nor the right being the same again." At that time, Aron wrote political articles for "Combat," an intellectual journal, but he wrote them as a philosophy professor would, as one who "wanted to prove that he could be a publicist as well." Characterizing the political situation in France in the beginning of 1946, he concluded that there existed "three coalitions: on the one hand there were communists, on the other, anti-communists, and the third coalition was made up of only one individual: General de Gaulle." When it finally came to an altercation between the coalitions, the great loser among them turned out to be the last of the three. "He did not want to govern France through a parliament, or lead discussions and unending negotiations with political parties."

At this time, all of Europe was faced with the problem of post war political and territorial divisions. To answer the question "did there exist the possibility of challenging the USSR's consequent occupation of Eastern Europe in 1945–1946?" – Aron stated that without the Americans it was not possible since "the Americans immediately demobilized their army." As a result, only one half of Europe was "Sovietised, but the other half could rebuild with the help of Americans. "Some French believe to this day that the influence that Americans had on Western Europe is comparable to the influence – if it can be labelled as such! – that the Soviets had on the Eastern part of the continent." A later part of these statements provided the following arguments for the formulation of Aron's general thesis, that post war France had in fact not one but two political opponents, meaning the United States and the USSR. In his opinion, they both share responsibility for the fact that "France was demoted to a purely regional power."

The second part of the interview, covering the years 1947–1956, is titled: *Democracy and Totalitarianism.* Aron had then become affiliated with "Figaro," considered in France to be a right wing journal, as well as with the right wing of the political scene, in his case the Gaulistic RPF (Rassemblement du Peuple Français). In this conversation, it was brought up that in 1951 he published the

[32] Ibidem, p. 98.

book *Chain Reaction Wars* [Les Guerres en Chaîne], in which he urged "Europe to abandon its defensive strategy." His reply was that this strategy resulted in the USSR being, among others, "an economic disaster, a great military power, and possibly a large colonial empire." As a member of the RPF, Aron supported its activists, who opposed the creation of the coalition government with the communists. It was also brought up that in 1955 he published a book titled *The Opium of the Intellectuals*, in which he analysed "the mythology of the left-wing intelligentsia" while criticising these intellectuals for staying under Soviet communism's spell. On the other hand, Aron reminded others of his indication that the US was that real power which as a member of NATO could effectively challenge communism. He added to this that "the mercantilized American society can be hated, but American civilization itself is liberal. If the US had any influence on Europe, it would be in the sense of imparting liberal institutions, dear to the hearts of most intellectuals."[33] This is one of his few amicable statements addressing the United States, and also clear declarations on the side of liberalism.

[33] Cf. ibidem, p. 166.

Chapter 7

Liberalism and democracy

Not every form of democracy may be reconciled with liberal ideas and postulates. Moreover, some of them move away from liberalism to such an extent that it can be said that there exist both liberal and non-liberal democracies. This became especially apparent following the formation of the so-called people's democracies, i.e. those that came into being in the second half of the 20th century. However, at the beginning of that century a completely different approach might still have seemed obvious, according to which there was no liberalism without democracy or democracy without liberalism. Liberals themselves could have somehow contributed to this attitude since they frequently used the terms *liberalism* and *democracy* in a way which might have led to the conclusion that they were synonymous. Also, authors writing about liberalism and democracy played a role here. For many of them, liberalism and democracy were mutually complementary.[1] And even those who, like Guido de Ruggiero, were aware of both similarities and differences between the two, maintained that the latter were in fact minor in character.[2]

---

[1] One of these authors is John H. Hallowell. He claims that "Historically considered, the relationship between liberalism and democracy is an intimate one; for modern democratic government and liberalism developed concomitantly. Both have their roots in the seventeenth century; and, ever since the seventeenth century, democracy as a form of government has been sustained by liberalism as a political and social philosophy." Cf. J. H. Hallowell, *The Moral Foundation of Democracy*, Chicago 1954, p. 68.

[2] G. de Ruggiero claims that "the principles lying at the root of the democratic idea are a logical development of the ideal premisses of modern liberalism. They may be summarised in two formulae: the extension of individual rights to all members of the community, and the right of the people as an organic whole to govern itself." He also states that nowadays "Liberalism and the new form of democracy have come to coincide in their formal conception of the

Giovanni Sartori, however, in his *Democratic Theory*, came to a different general conclusion. Namely, he placed emphasis not on the term *liberalism* but on *democracy* – a term which, in his view, is easier to define than the former. Naturally, the fact that it was easier to define did not mean that it was easy to comprehend. Its etymological analysis already shows a high degree of ambiguity in its meaning has. The word democracy comes from Greek and consists of two elements, the first of which is *demos*, which signifies *people*, and the other is *kratos*, which means *power*. Thus, the word *democracy* means *the power of the people.* The problem is that both in the past and at present the two elements of the word have been and are ambiguous in character. "*Demos* in the fifth century B.C. meant the Athenian community gathered in the *ekklesia.* However, even thus defined, *demos* can be reduced to *plethos*, that is, the *plenum*, the entire body; or to the *polloi*, the many; or to the *pléiones*, the majority; or to *óchlos*, the mob (this being a degenerative meaning). And the moment *demos* is translated into modern language the ambiguities increase. The Italian term *popolo*, as well as its French and German equivalents (*peuple*, *Volk*) convey the idea of a singular entity, whereas the English word *people* indicates a plural."[3] Difficulties increase further when we approach the problem of the links between the terms people and power as well as *demos* and *kratos.*

John Locke attempted to deal with the same issue in yet another way. He explained the relationship between liberalism and democracy in the context of his discussion of government. In his second treatise on this issue, he began by depicting the situation of a man living in the state of nature and then came to outlining his situation as a member of a political community. According to him, at the beginning of this path, people live in "a state of perfect freedom to order their actions, and dispose of their possessions and persons," and "state also of equality, wherein all the power and jurisdiction is reciprocal, no one having more than another." However, at the end of this path, freedom already becomes limited by positive laws, while the supreme power remains in the hands of the legislature – all of this was meant for the common good and happening with the voluntary consent of the individuals constituting that community. It is only then that Lock raises the issue of democracy. In his Chapter X entitled *Of the Forms of the Commonwealth*, he points to a situation in which "the majority having, as has been shewed, upon men's first uniting into

State, a conception based on the recognition of individual rights and the people's capacity for self-government. The democratic extension of liberal principles has its practical complement in the extension of political rights to all citizens, and the administration of the lower social orders into the lower social classes..." Cf. G. de Ruggiero, *The History of European Liberalism*, Boston 1959, p. 371 ff.

[3] Cf. G. Sartori, *Democratic Theory*, Detroit 1962, p. 17 ff.

society, the whole power of the community naturally in them, may employ all that power in making laws for the community from time to time, and executing those laws by officers of their own appointing; and then the form of the government is a perfect democracy." His further arguments imply that we can talk about democracy only when the supreme, i.e. legislative power, belongs to the community.

Therefore, it is necessary to answer the question what is really meant by the term *community*. Locke explained that he understood the term *community* as "any independent community, which the Latines signified by the word civitas, to which the word which best answers in our language, is commonwealth..."[4] However, neither *civitas* nor *commonwealth* refers to a community of all the people living in a given country. Neither does it refer to all those who somehow cope with their own lives. Locke actually puts more stress on independence. What this really means was to some extent shown by all those battles for religious and political independence from the Anglican Church and the King of England. Obviously, all this gave the idea of democracy a specific local colour. I am inclined to claim, however, that just as there is no liberalism as such, there is also no such thing as democracy in general. Any combination of these two always results in something that is tailor-made for a concrete place and time. For this reason, it is difficult to hold a reasonable discussion on the issue of democracy without relating it to that particular place and time.

As a matter of fact, the above assumptions are far from revealing. Alexis de Tocqueville already followed this line of argument in his *Democracy in America*. He was neither interested in the etymological complexities of the term *democracy* nor any theoretical analysis of the possibilities of its use. What did interest him, however, was *democracy in action*, i.e. democracy in its natural and cultural circumstances, its intentions, aims, successes, failures and limitations. What is characteristic of his book is that in the first volume he avoided overusing the term *democracy*, not only due to its ambiguous meaning but also because his understanding of democracy was at odds with the social realities of the feudal France he presented. The second volume is completely different in this respect. Not only does Tocqueville use the term in each of its chapters, but also he uses it in so many different contexts and combines it with issues that are so different, and at the same time vital for social life, that one can easily come to the conclusion that without democracy this life would not be possible at all.[5]

---

[4] Cf. J. Locke, *Two Treatises of Government*, New York 1963, p. 400.

[5] For example, in Chapter II of Part One he talks about "beliefs among democratic peoples," in Chapter V in the same Part he mentions "democratic instincts" and in Chapter VII "the mind of democratic peoples." In Part Two there is a mention of, among other things, "individualism in democratic countries," the "well-understood interest" of Americans, their

Robert David Putnam followed the same approach to democracy in the 1970s in his book under a meaningful title *Making Democracy Work: Civic Traditions in Modern Italy*. In its Introduction he wrote that "this book aims to contribute to our understanding of the performance of democratic institutions." He called the scientific method used for this the "soaking and poking" and added that it "requires the researcher to marinate herself in the minutiae of an institution." He limited the area of this "soaking and poking" to selected regions of Northern and Middle Italy. Thus, it is impossible to briefly and unambiguously answer the question: how does this affect liberalism and democracy? The conclusions are many and they vary in their degree of generality and importance.[6] But I am inclined to share the point of view of those who admit that in certain respects Putnam's conclusions converge with those drawn by A. de Tocqueville. Does this mean that the societies of Western Europe have Americanised themselves? I do not think so. Rather, this means that liberal democracies, which can be found both in Europe and North America, possess such elements that can be called their "backbone." It sometimes leans to the left and sometimes to the right but, all the same, it still manages to support the structure referred to as Western political culture.

1. Liberal democracies

The above-mentioned "backbone" can be regarded as the absolute minimum of democracy and liberalism since, without it, democracy would cease to be democracy, and liberalism would no longer be liberalism. Naturally, these minima were different in character depending on the given place and time since both democracy and liberalism have always been involved in some concrete social reality. However, one could attempt not only to articulate them but also to show the relationships existing between them. Giovanni Sartori was one of those who made such an attempt. In his aforementioned monograph, he depicts liberty and equality as categories which make it possible to talk about liberal democracies; "liberalism calls for liberty and democracy for equality. To unite them, we say that it is the task of liberal-democratic systems to combine

"excessive love of well-being" as well as "exalted spiritualism," etc. Cf. A. de Tocqueville, *Democracy in America*, vol. II, Chicago 2000.

[6] For example "[...] the performance of representative government is facilitated by the social infrastructure of civic communities and by the democratic values of both officials and citizens. Most fundamental to the civic community is the social ability to collaborate for shared interests. [...] The harmonies of a choral society illustrate how voluntary collaboration can create value that no individual, no matter how wealthy, no matter how wily, could produce alone." Cf. R.D. Putnam, *Making Democracy Work: Civic Traditions in Modern Italy*, Princeton, p. 182 ff.

liberty with equality." That it is possible to combine liberty with equality is proved by the fact that Western-style systems are both liberal and democratic. However, this is where the unquestionable issues end. Further on, doubts arise. Sartori himself admits to this by stating that "liberal democracy can be viewed as a skein with two ends. As long as the skein is not touched, all is well, but if we begin to pull the ends and unravel it, we see that it is made up of two different-colored threads."[7] In his view, the solution to this problem is to come down from the high level of theoretical discussion and move on towards "a more concrete level." At this level, the difference between liberalism and democracy lies in the fact that "liberalism is above all the technique of limiting the State's power, whereas democracy is the insertion of popular power into the State."[8] Though this does not make it possible to roll up this "skein" in order to make it a unified whole, at least it makes it possible to find some logic and consistency in this act of "pulling" its two opposite ends.

Personally, I suggest following this attitude towards a liberal democracy. Unlike Sartori, however, I am of the opinion that this "sein" consists of a larger number of essential elements and that, obviously, it has more than two ends which can be pulled, depending on specific social needs and opportunities. This not only means that, practically, there exist many different liberal democracies but also that, despite fundamental differences between them, it is possible to distinguish between those which are liberal and those which are not. This distinction requires coming down from the level of general ideas, principles and postulates and moving towards concrete areas in which democracy manifests itself in action. In order to avoid any confusion, it is necessary to begin with the highest level and then to gradually come down to lower levels.

This approach was adopted by, among others, John Rawls in his *Theory of Justice* (1971). He placed two principles of justice at the highest level of generality (in his view, liberal democracy is a set of "principles of social justice"):

– the first of these states that "each person is to have an equal right to the most extensive scheme of equal basic liberties compatible with a similar scheme of liberties for others;"

---

[7] "If we pull the liberal thread, not every form of equality disappears; but liberal equality, as such, is above all intended to promote, by way of liberty, qualitative aristocracies. Liberalism per se is wary of granting more than juridico-political equality..." Cf. G. Sartori, *Democratic Theory*, op. cit., p. 368. However, too sharp a pull on "the thread of democracy" leads, as already indicated by Émile Faguet, to "the cult of incompetence" or, in a slightly milder form, "the cult of mediocrity" (Ruggiero wrote about this in his aforementioned monograph).

[8] A little later he adds that "The liberal is on the defensive on the social plane, but is active when it comes to supervising the method of creating the social order. The democrat is somewhat indifferent to method, is concerned above all with substance, and prefers exercising power (in the redistributive sense) to watching over it." G. Sartori, *Democratic Theory*, op. cit., p. 370.

– the second states that "social and economic inequalities are to be arranged so that they are both (a) reasonably expected to be to everyone's advantage, and (b) attached to positions and offices open to all..."[9]

Next, he explains that he refers here to the basic liberties of citizens and that for him these liberties are "political liberty (the right to vote and to hold public office) and freedom of speech and assembly; liberty of conscience and freedom of thought; freedom of the person, which includes freedom from psychological oppression and physical assault and dismemberment (integrity of the person); the right to hold personal property and freedom from arbitrary arrest and seizure as defined by the concept of the rule of law. These liberties are to be equal by the first principle [...]. The second principle applies, in the first approximation, to the distribution of income and wealth and to the design of organizations that make use of differences in authority and responsibility." Further on, the author of this work, which has been acclaimed as a kind of manifesto of liberal democracy (it should be added: American-style democracy), continues his clarification of the theory of social justice by delving into the complex structure of its secondary, tertiary, and so on, principles.[10]

Any analysis of the foundations of liberal democracy leads, or at least should lead, to raising the issue of the relationship between the citizen and the state. Scholars who, like Locke in the past and Rawls, who is mentioned above, as well as other leading representatives of the contemporary approach to American liberalism (e.g. Walter Lipmann or Daniel Bell), expose the role of the citizen and minimise the role of the state at the same time. Their general view in this respect can be summarised as follows: "the less of the state and the more of the citizen, the better both for the citizen and for the state." In the past, this statement functioned under the name *laissez faire* or under the term "a night watchman state" (i.e. a state which only makes sure that its citizens respect the law and so "does not poke its nose into" its citizens' matters). Nowadays, its extreme form exists under the name libertarianism, with one of its leading representatives being Robert Nozick, the author of *Anarchy, State, and Utopia* (1974). In this book, he praises an individual not merely as a citizen but as an individual who can "plan their lives in the long run" and who can "choose to refrain from actions which would upset the pattern." At the same time, it praises the state "limited to the narrow functions of protection against force, theft, fraud and enforcement of contracts."[11] It is an undeniable

[9] Cf. J. Rawls, *A Theory of Justice*, Cambridge 1999, p. 53.

[10] By way of indicating how complex this structure is, let me just add that in its second row are the following principles: for a community – efficiency and differentiation, and for individuals – reliability and natural duties; in the third: "averaged utility," "limited participation," "tolerance intolerance," etc.

[11] Cf. R. Nozick, *Anarchy, State, and Utopia*, Oxford 1991, p. ix ff.

fact that this approach towards the citizen and the state contains elements of liberal ideology. The question remains, however, whether it has sufficiently preserved these assumptions and postulates, without which democracy ceases to be democracy.

According to European political thought, such a considerable reduction in the role of the state is usually associated more with anarchism than with liberalism. Even Isaiah Berlin, an advocate of the concept of negative freedom (liberty "from..."), did not limit the role of the state to that of a policeman giving drivers parking tickets. Even if European liberals used to claim that the state was evil by its very nature (since in each case it imposed various limitations on man and the citizen), they would add to this that it was a necessary evil (without it the citizen would not feel secure enough to leave their home). They did notice many problems occurring between the citizen and the state but, at the same time, they were convinced that it was possible to solve them without doing any harm either to the citizen or to the state. In their view, they could offer so many solutions that, consequently, one could talk about numerous models of liberal democracy.[12]

One of the most interesting of these solutions was suggested by Friedrich August von Hayek (1899–1992). Born and educated in Vienna, where he studied law, psychology and economics, Hayek spent much of his professional life in England where, between 1931 and 1950, he lectured at the London School of Economics, and in the United States, where he held the position of professor in several universities between the years 1950 and 1962. In 1974, together with another economist, Gunnar Myrdal, he received the Nobel Memorial Prize for his achievements in Economic Sciences.[13]

Hayek was an outspoken opponent of conservatism who supported liberalism. In his *Constitution of Liberty*, he presented his views by stating that "the conservative and the liberal dispositions differ radically. As has often been acknowledged by conservative writers, one of the fundamental traits of the conservative attitude is a fear of change, a timid distrust of the new as such,

[12] In literature they are frequently reduced to two major ones, i.e. to the model of procedural democracy (where stress is put on "legal procedures which regulate the activity of the authorities, the institution of the state as well as the ways in which citizens achieve their goals"), and the model of a republican democracy (where stress is put on who exerts power and in what way). Cf. W. Kaczocha, *Demokracja proceduralna oraz republikańska* [Procedural and Republican Democracy], Poznan 2004. In my opinion, this division is not wrong but rather too simplified to render the reality of liberal democracies in contemporary Europe.

[13] He is the author of treatises on economy (such as, e.g. *The Pure Theory of Capital*, 1941) and on philosophy as well as Political Sciences, such as *The Constitution of Liberty* (1960), and *Law, Legislation and Liberty* (vol. 1–3, 1973–1979), *The Road to Serfdom (1944)*, *The Counter-Revolution of Science: Studies on the Reason* (1952), and *The Fatal Conceit: the Errors of Socialism* (1988).

while the liberal position is based on courage and confidence, on a preparedness to let change run its course even if we cannot predict where it will lead. [...] But the conservatives are inclined to use the powers of government to prevent change or to limit its rate to whatever appeals to the more timid mind. In looking forward, they lack the faith in the spontaneous forces of adjustment which makes the liberal accept changes without apprehension, even though he does not know how the necessary adaptations will be brought about. It is, indeed, part of the liberal attitude to assume that, especially in the economic field, the self-regulating forces of the market will somehow bring about the required adjustments to new conditions, although no one can foretell how they will do this in a particular instance. [...] The conservative feels safe and content only if he is assured that some higher wisdom watches and supervises change, only if he knows that some authority is charged with keeping the change 'orderly.'"[14] In brief, the conservative is someone who, in the relationship between the state and the citizen, opts for the state, while the liberal is the one who favours the citizen.

Such a dualistic division of the political scene corresponds to the reality of contemporary Europe to a lesser degree than to that of the United States of America, where the conservatives are associated with the Republican Party and the liberals with the Democratic Party. Naturally, members of both of the parties consider themselves to be democratic. The problem is that they differ in their understanding of democracy. Similarly, even in England the traditional political division into the Tories, who promote conservative ideas, and the Whigs, who support liberalism, has become out-of-date to a great extent. This was caused, above all, by the introduction of socialism as an ideology and a political option which unified the political powers dissatisfied both with conservatism and liberalism.

Obviously, Hayek was well-aware of all the above. In his aforementioned *Constitution of Liberty* he claimed that, in order to outline the image of the main political powers, it is necessary to draw a diagram in the form of a triangle – "with the socialists on the left, the conservatives on the right, and the liberals somewhere in the middle." He emphasised, however, that "socialists have for a long time been able to pull harder," while "the conservatives have tended to follow the socialist rather than the liberal idea and have adopted at appropriate intervals of time those ideas made respectable by radical propaganda." This applies, among other things, to the idea of central planning and the top-down state control of changes taking place in social life.

---

[14] F.A. Hayek, *The Constitution of Liberty*, Chicago 1978, p. 400 ff.

Already in his article from 1937, entitled *Social Calculation I: The Nature and the History of the Problem*, Hayek argued (following another Austrian economist, Ludwig von Mises) that socialist economic thought opted not for – as was in the case of the market economy – the activity, creativity and economic entrepreneurship of those particular entities which are involved in the game of competition, but for the possibly accurate valuation of all the elements engaged (directly or indirectly) in the process of the production of goods as well as for the precise planning of both production and distribution. For this purpose, what is needed is a planner that will not only possess the competence of an engineer managing the production or of a tradesman dealing with the distribution but also of a scholar acquainted with the social conditions as well as a politician deciding on the direction of social changes.[15]

Hayek did not claim that socialists accepted the possibility of the existence of such a social planner who, like God, knows everything and can do everything. He did claim, however, that they brought into existence state institutions, such as, for example, the Central Planning Office, which carries out all the particular tasks assigned by that planner and where there appear those who call for "a central direction of all economic activity according to a single plan, laying down how the resources of society should be "consciously directed" to serve particular ends in a definite way."[16]

The problem lies not only in that, essentially, the above-mentioned purposes are not able to be performed, but also in the fact that it enables such planners to enslave all those whom they force to carry out their plans in various ways. It is also a way for the state to replace the citizen and to introduce justice which is regulated centrally ("in a short time it will no longer be about who 'deserves' what, but everything will be reduced to the 'political necessity' which will determine which group is to be favoured at the expense of the community"). It is also a way for those in power to free themselves from social control. These are not the only negative effects which Hayek points out in his criticism of socialism and central planning.[17] Still, the effects themselves are a sufficient justification for the general conclusion that this ideology, philosophy and social politics has little in common with the democracy promoted by

[15] "Economic control," he wrote, "is not merely control of a sector of human life which can be separated from the rest; it is the control of the means for all our means. And whoever has sole control of the means must also determine which ends are to be served." F. A. Hayek, *The Road to Serfdom*, London 2006, p. 95.

[16] Ibidem, p. 36.

[17] For more information cf. W. Banach, *Spontaniczność a planowanie. Wokół filozofii społecznej Friedricha A. von Hayeka* [Spontaneity and Planning. About the Social Philosophy of Friedrich A. von Hayek], Poznan 2003 (especially Chapter III).

liberals. This is so because the latter opt not only for the spontaneous activity undertaken by each particular citizen but also for the market economy, as well as constantly and to a greater extent reducing the role of the state in social life.[18] It has to be added, though, that according to the author of *The Constitution of Liberty,* this reduction should not lead to limiting its function to that of the duties of the guardian of public order. In his opinion, even in very liberal democracies, the state will have to "provide such conditions in which individuals and groups will be able to aim at the more effective realisation of their aims, even if this sometimes meant using means of coercion in order to obtain income necessary to provide the services which, for various reasons, the market cannot provide."[19]

2. Non-liberal democracies

It is obvious that, from the point of view of liberals, communist governments have little in common with liberalism. It is not so obvious, however, whether communism has anything to do with democracy. The fact that these governments use the term *democracy* to define a specific political system like the so-called people's democracy does not mean that the use of the term is not an abuse in this case. If we assume, solely on the basis of the etymology of the term, that democracy is the same as the reign of the common people, then we have these "common people" (identified with the urban and the rural proletariat) in power, not only by means of their declarations but also through representative, government and local government political bodies. The problem is, however, that even though they are members of those bodies, they do not have decision-making power but executive power only.

Michał Heller and Aleksander Niekricz claimed, in their monograph on the birth of the Soviet Union, that when the communists were coming into power in Russia they not only had a lot to say but they also had a lot to do. And they did much, first by selecting Councils of Workers' and Soldiers' Delegates and then by brutally dealing with their class enemies. It soon turned out, however, that "the proletariat of towns and villages" and their political leaders had differed in the way they imagined that rule was to be in the future. Naturally, the former wanted the power to go down to as low a level as possible, while

---

[18] "Liberalism consciously limits the control of the state over the general social order to the enforcement of the compliance with general rules, which are necessary to create spontaneous order, whose details are unpredictable." F. A. Hayek, *Law, Legislation and Liberty*, vol. I, Chicago 1973, p. 32.

[19] Ibidem, vol. III, p. 139.

the latter did their best for the power to go up to the highest possible level even though they declaratively subscribed to the proletariat's postulates.[20] The problems with the exercising of power by "the avant-garde of the working class" (as the communist leaders called themselves) began to accumulate due to it being threatened by a counter-revolution, the misery of those working the hardest and, finally, due to the open discontent of those whom those leaders had owed and had promised so much. Therefore, they had to give up their democratic slogans and announce the proletariat's dictatorship instead. When asked how this concept should be understood, Lenin would answer that dictatorship meant "unlimited power, based on force and not on law." In theory, this meant concentrating all the power in the hands of one social class (the proletariat). In practice, on the other hand, all the power was first accumulated in the hands of a small group of its prominent leaders and later, during the so-called Stalin era, in the hands of one man.[21]

Undoubtedly, even if democracy is understood in its broadest sense, it is difficult to reconcile such a state of affairs with democracy – but not a declarative democracy but one which is put into practice and in which its ordinary citizens can feel that they enjoy the benefits derived from it.[22] Also, the real life of communist countries has always had little in common with the Kingdom

---

[20] The aforementioned authors of the history of the Soviet Union point to the characteristic evolution of the views of Lenin himself – in the booklet *The State and the Revolution* he claimed that only "a hopeless ignorant and a bourgeois con man can maintain that blue-collar workers are able to manage industry and the state." M. Heller, A. Niekricz, *Utopia u władzy. Historia Związku Sowieckiego* [Utopia in Power. The History of the Soviet Union], vol. 1, Wroclaw 1989, p. 47.

[21] What the people's democracy looked like in that era, i.e. 1945–1953, is described by, among others, François Fejtö. Its main achievement was the Sovietisation of Central and Eastern European countries by imposing the Soviet model of management and exercise of power. This expressed itself in the state's taking control (under the slogans of the so-called agricultural reform and nationalisation) over its economy, liquidating socialist parties and submitting communist parties to Moscow, taking measures to repress Churches as well as imposing central planning in all the spheres of social life. Cf. F. Fejtö, *Histoire des démocriaties populaires*, vol. 1, Paris 1979.

[22] Heller and Niekricz, in their *Utopia and Power* point out that even Stalin's Constitution from 1936 "in fact gave its Soviet citizens democratic rights: freedom of speech, assembly, the press, demonstration as well as freedom of mass meeting, religious worship, anti-religious propaganda, inviolability of the dwelling and confidentiality of correspondence. There was no right to freedom of movement but, instead, all the citizens were granted the right to vote – the category of people called *lishency* was liquidated and there were to be secret-ballot, direct and equal elections" (cf. ibidem, vol. 1, p. 234). What this really looked like in practice is described by these two authors and the aforementioned authors of *The Black Book of Communism* (e.g. in chapters *Socially Foreign Elements and the Cycles of Repression*, *The Great Terror* and *The Empire of the Camps*).

of Freedom which the ideological founding fathers of Marxism had promised. Although some of the poorest social classes had indeed been liberated from their inhumane working and living conditions such as the ones described by Friedrich Engels in his *The Condition of the Working Class in England*, these same and other groups had, at the same time, become enslaved by the communist system, based on repression and the omnipresent fear of the law enforcement and control apparatus used for imposing so-called "class" justice. It must be clearly stated, therefore, that Lenin, before he came into power, had serious doubts whether the communists should promise that Kingdom to those social masses.[23] Stalin, on the other hand, after he had concentrated all this power in his hands, saw too many class and personal enemies near him and so was too preoccupied with dealing with them to find time to concern himself with something as esoteric as the "Kingdom of Freedom."

Nowadays, it is obvious that Soviet communism and Western European socialism are one and the same. Before, however, the two went separate ways, and socialists themselves were quite confused in this respect. This was so because both communists and socialists referred to Marxism, which seemed to them a scientific and extensively documented theory of social life. One of the characteristic features of this theory was that it was possible to interpret it in a variety of ways. As a result, there was and there is still, as it seems, no single Marxism nowadays. Quite the opposite – there are so many of them that it is difficult to unambiguously answer the question which of them is closest to the thought of Marx himself.[24] Leszek Kołakowski in his *Main Currents of Marxism* presents the different varieties of Marxism and its different links with socialism as well. In his view, "only in Germany was it possible [...] to frame and maintain for a considerable time a uniform ideology based on Marxist premisses, or what were generally regarded as such." It exerted relatively little influence on English socialism, which was mainly inspired by R. Owen's, J. Bentham's and J.S. Mill's thoughts.[25] It is worth mentioning here the fact that, according to

[23] Undoubtedly, these are mentioned already in his letter from 1875 to Bebl, where he claimed that "it is pure nonsense to talk of a 'free people's State;' so long as the proletariat still uses the State it does not use it in the interest of freedom but in order to hold down its adversaries, and as soon as it becomes possible to speak of freedom the State as such ceases to exist." Cited by G. Sartori, *Democratic Theory*, op.cit., p. 447.

[24] According to Józef Maria Bocheński, there is no one possible right "insight" into Marx's views. However, it is possible, and even necessary, to differentiate between Marxism and communism – the author claims that "The real creator of communism is Włodziemierz Iljicz Uljanow (1870–1924), who assumed the pseudonym 'Lenin' while in exile in Siberia." Cf. J.M. Bocheński *Lewica, religia, sowietologia* [The Left, Religion, Sovietology], Warsaw 1996, p. 96.

[25] Cf. L. Kołakowski, *Main Currents of Marxism: Its Rise, Growth, and Dissolution*, vol. 2, London 1978, p. 1 ff.

John Gray, socialism had and has more in common with conservatism than with communism ("socialist thought echoes conservative voices in lamenting the dislocation of ancient folkways brought about by commerce and industry") and that the representatives of both of these political options formed one front in their fight against the individualism which liberalism strongly promoted.[26] Anyway, the emergence of, first, Bolshevism and then communism caused that Western European socialism started to more and more clearly distance itself from revolutionary slogans as well as revolutionary practice, and to rely more on evolutionary (peaceful) changes as well as a democratic country.

In England, members of the Fabian Society (founded in 1884) such as Beatrice and Sidney Webb, George Bernard Shaw and Annie Besant, encouraged the English to follow the same path. They raised their voices in defence of the poorest part of society (by postulating e.g. the introduction of taxes whose amount would depend on income) and a democratic country (by postulating e.g. the reduction of the electoral threshold). Those who were more radical (called "anarcho-syndicalists" or "guildists") called for the foundation of so-called "guilds," i.e. social organisations whose activity combined the function of trade unions and the function of labour councils. The Fabian Society led to the formation of the Labour Party in England in 1900, a political party which has had unquestionable achievements both in defending the world of workers and the Western European democracy. The same can be said about Social Democracy in other countries, whose multiple, sometime even long-term coalitions of their governments with liberals confirm that nowadays they are definitely closer to liberalism than to Marxism.[27]

Obviously, this does not mean that the differences between liberal and socialist democracies have become completely blurred. Generally, what differentiates them is the thing which has always distinguished them, i.e. their attitude towards the state and the citizen. Naturally, liberals would not like the state to prevent its citizens from reaching their lifetime goals. Contemporary socialists, on the other hand, require that the state supports its citizens where this is necessary and possible. They believe that the scope of this support is still considerable. Today, it is not only, and above all, about financial support for the poorest or giving them a job but also about helping numerous people in their intellectual development (by e.g. providing them with a chance to

---

[26] "Like conservatives, socialists rejected [...] the abstract individualism of liberal thought and the liberal ideas of the state of civil society in favour of the concept of moral community." J. Gray, *Liberalism. Essays in Political Philosophy*, New York 1989, p. 103 ff.

[27] It is worth mentioning here that even German socio-democrats so closely "related" with Marxism decided to definitely distance themselves from Marxism in its SPD programme submitted at the 1959 congress in Godesberg.

receive an education) and in their moral development (by e.g. inculcating into them proper patterns of behaviour).[28] From the sociological point of view, the state is not only "a great nanny" but also "a great lawmaker" and a guardian of the law – for a Social Democrat it is law which the majority of the citizens want. The fact that most people today want such law that guarantees liberty, equality, justice and many other individual and group values is so obvious to a Social Democrat that he will refuse to discuss this issue with a liberal. Finally, for a socialist, the state is also "a great householder," i.e. the one who can plan housekeeping well and who can equally well implement plans, seeing to it that each citizen, both rich and poor, can derive tangible benefits from this. Of course, these benefits cannot be the same (as in communism) but neither can they be divided in such a way (as in "wild" capitalism) that the former will not know what to do with excess while the latter will have a deep conviction that they have been cheated. A liberal may frown upon this as he is convinced that if a poor citizen cannot help himself, no one and nothing will support him in realising his lifetime ambitions. Neither will the state, even when it is a democratic one. However, even he has to agree that those like-minded ones belong to the social minority. The majority are those who have to be helped in various ways. This might be a factor in explaining the fact that the Western European liberal parties, unlike the Social Democratic parties, are not massive in character and do not enjoy massive social support, either.

[28] So-called ethical socialism puts special emphasis on this last issue. Cf. P. Self, *Political Theories of Moderns Government*, London 1985.

Chapter 8

The moral ideals of liberalism

In the case of every significant social ideology, the ideal is to achieve the virtues they point to. This is how liberalism understands the case. The problem is that the concept of *virtue* also has many meanings, just like the term *liberalism.* This consequently could not and cannot lead to clear meanings when indicating which virtues a liberal can and should cultivate. This did not deter them, however, from looking for diverse virtues, to organize them and present them as a unique moral code for liberalism. An attempt to create such a code is, for example, Montesquieu's *The Spirit of the Laws.* In his dissertation, the author poses the question "what is virtue in a political system?" and states that it "is a most simple thing: it is a love of the republic; it is a sensation, and not a consequence of acquired knowledge: a sensation that may be felt by the most miserable person [...] in the state."

As the discussion unfolds, however, the issue becomes more complex. It turns out that the love of the republic is a love of democracy as well as a love of modesty and equality, and this in turn is revealed to be the love of good sense and happiness of citizens which "largely consists in their having middling talents and fortunes."[1] What is more, it also turns out that this list of virtues has to be extended by the love of honour and various kinds of class privileges. The image of the virtues enumerated by Montesquieu becomes even more complex in these fragments of *The Spirit of the Laws* where he points to specific situations concerning virtuous (or non-virtuous) behaviour. It is clear that one cannot deem virtuous the conduct of a despotic monarch who enforces obedience on his subjects. It is also clear (at least for Montesquieu) that it is not virtuous

[1] Cf. Montesquieu, *The Spirit of the Laws*, Cambridge 2006, p. 44.

for the subjects in a despotic state to present their monarch with gifts out of fear of him.[2] It is not clear, however, whether it is a virtue to support female administration (discussed in book VII chapter 17 of *The Spirit of the Laws*).

A modern attempt to define liberal morality by indicating a catalogue of its accepted and propagated virtues can be found in Stephen Macedo's dissertation entitled *Liberal Virtues*. In the introduction the author states: "at best the expression *liberal virtues* may seem a contradiction in terms and may even be a dangerous invitation to government intervention, political perfectionism and paternalism. Liberals used to say that the government should not strive to make people virtuous; it should only guarantee equal freedom, order, security and a few other widely accepted public values. To a large extent I agree with this." A bit later, however, he adds that "liberal politics requires a certain level and quality of civic virtue and living in a reasonably just, tolerant and open political system supports the development of this virtue in many respects."[3] This does not only mean advocating the need to make use of specific liberal virtues, but also indicating a few of them – such as reasonable justice, tolerance or system openness. On the one hand, it is a reference to the classical understanding of virtues (based on Aristotle's *Nicomachean Ethics*), on the other, a reference to its understanding by modern and contemporary liberals (such as the one presented in Karl R. Popper's *The Open Society and Its Enemies*).[4]

It must, however, be emphasized that these references are rather loose and – equally important – fairly detached from both the classical and non-classical understanding of virtues. It is a consequence of Macedo's conviction that, while liberal virtues "are models of perfection, specific to citizens of liberal systems, capable of flourishing in a society created by liberalism," at the same time "utterly utopian and unrealistic expectations should be avoided." An example of such an expectation would be the assumption that there will be no major difference between the models of civic and government perfection and the citizens living in given societies. Later in his dissertation the author clearly demonstrates that it is not only citizens who are imperfect, but also various ideologies, including the moral ideology of liberalism. However,

[2] "In a republic, presents are odious, because virtue stands in no need of them. In monarchies, honour is a much stronger incentive than presents. But in a despotic government, where there is neither honour nor virtue, people cannot be determined to act but through hope of the conveniences of life." Ibidem, p. 65.

[3] Cf. S. Macedo, *Cnoty liberalne* [Liberal Virtues. Citizenship, Virtue and Community], Cracow 1995, p. 13 ff. Idem, *Liberal Virtues. Citizenship, Virtue and Community*, Oxford 1990.

[4] In *Nicomachean Ethics* Aristotle considers cultivating virtue to be the superior aim of human life. He also states there that "human virtue is the one in which the working of reason participates," which means that there is no true morality without true rationality and vice versa. Cf. Aristotle, *Etyka nikomachejska* [Nicomachean Ethics], Warsaw 2000, p. 88 ff.

an attempt to escape from the moral ideology of liberalism in the form of communitarian ideology (represented for instance by Michael Sandel) is not perfect either.[5] Obviously, this does not hamper the discussion on the moral ideas of liberalism, but prevents one from discussing them as precisely such ideas which match each and every action of a citizen who considers himself a liberal. These moral ideas can and should be a form of encouragement to achieve a specified kind of perfection as well as point to the path leading to this achievement. At any rate, this is the sense in which I am discussing the moral ideas of liberalism.

All moral ideas indicated here are based on the belief that for a liberal who is conscious of his vocation, objectives and place on the social map, there is no freedom without morality and no morality without virtue. These virtues include tolerance, rational egoism, calculated altruism, responsibility and a predictability of behaviour. The first three I consider cardinal while the last two complement them directly. I would not object, however, if one thinks of them as equally important as the ones mentioned in the first place. The following list is also in no sense exhaustive.

1. Tolerance

Tolerance is postulated by both past and contemporary liberals. In general, they say more or less the same things that are expressed in *A Letter Concerning Toleration* [...] *from a Friend of Peace, Enemy of Persecution, John Locke, and Englishman*. The title itself states that what people need is not war but peace. This cannot be achieved without tolerance, that is, without accepting others' right to distinctness. It should be recalled that the author of the letter writes first of all about religious differences. Later liberals did not always want to remember about this and even when they did they rarely considered it worth emphasizing. Among them, Voltaire is the one who does not forget about it. In one of his *Letters Concerning the English Nation,* he expresses his admiration for Locke himself ("perhaps no man ever had a more judicious or more methodical genius, or was a more acute logician than Mr. Locke") and his work, at the same time severely criticising the worst "sanctimonious and superstitious" people who "loudly exclaimed that Mr. Locke intended to destroy religion; nevertheless, religion had nothing to do in the affair."[6]

[5] "Michael Sandel, a distinguished critic-communitarian, aims to attack 'deontological liberalism' based on the idea that 'conceptions of good are variegated and man is an entity who is not given their objectives but chooses them.'" S. Macedo, *Liberal Virtues...*, op. cit., p. 29 ff.

[6] Cf. Voltaire, *Letters Concerning the English Nation*, London 1778, pp. 86–87.

It is doubtful whether Voltaire was a careful reader of Locke's letter and if he correctly understood its message; and even if he understood it, whether he cultivated the tolerance advocated in Locke's treatise. When one analyses Voltaire's *Treatise on Tolerance* it becomes clear that it is possible to discuss tolerance and even write a laudatory hymn to it while at the same time remaining utterly intolerant towards any kinds of eccentrics (especially religious ones); not to mention such "trifles" as "love, gentleness and kindness towards all people in general" (these are moral virtues which for Locke constitute the direct complement of tolerance).[7]

Apart from all other issues, the way in which Vôltaire treats his opponents provokes a question concerning the limits of tolerance. This problem reappears in the writings of numerous liberals. None of them (including Locke) opted for limitless tolerance. Already in his introductory remarks to the treatise *On Liberty*, John Stuart Mill concentrates equally on civic liberty and the issue of various limits which a citizen has to take into account. If one is a liberal, then he obviously respects tolerance, although it is not easy and there is a strong temptation to be tolerant of himself and intolerant of others.[8] Sometimes liberals mistake tolerance for indifference or for not fully conscious hostility. Many such mistakes were committed by liberals at the time of the struggle to separate the Church from the state. However, it must be clearly stressed: today there is also no shortage of liberals who are willing to equate tolerance with indifference.[9] But this is not what this virtue is meant to be; of course, at least if tolerance is to remain a virtue and not, for instance, another social mystification.

What is tolerance all about and what it should mean are questions which are confronted in Michael Walzer's essay *On Toleration*. According to him, the contemporary social situation imposes previously unknown challenges and requirements on tolerance. Until recently, the measure of tolerance was its relation to other nationalities, especially to Jews. In the very beginning of the essay, Walzer announces: "As an American Jew, I grew up thinking of myself as an object of toleration." Although the USA is not Europe, in some European countries he notices changes which enforce a re-evaluation of the indicators of

[7] Cf. Voltaire, *Traktat o tolerancji napisany z powodu śmierci Jana Calasa* [Treatise on Tolerance On the Occasion of the Death of Jean Calas], Warsaw 1956.

[8] "So natural to mankind is intolerance in whatever they really care about, that religious freedom has hardly anywhere been practically achieved, except where religious indifference, which dislikes to have its peace disturbed by theological quarrels, has added its weight to the scale. In the minds of almost all religious persons, even in the most tolerant countries, the duty of toleration is admitted with tacit reserves." J. S. Mill, *On Liberty*, London 1867, p. 5.

[9] One of them is David Herzog. He openly suggests: "if religion has been causing social uproar for ages, let us treat it as if it did not have any political significance at all; it will thus lose its importance." Cf. D. Herzog, *Happy Slaves: A Critique of Consent Theory*, Chicago 1989, p. 165.

tolerance. First of all, he observes the emergence of such new phenomenon as an international community ("it is a very weak regime, but it is tolerant as a regime despite the intolerance of some of the states that make it up").

It is co-created, however, by national states. What poses a new challenge for tolerance in national states (such as, for example, France) is the appearance of numerous immigrant communities which isolate themselves from natives or which very poorly assimilate with them. Tolerance also has a specific character, because of the establishment of the European community called the European Union; "it requires its members to be more tolerant, and tolerant in different ways, than they have been in the past."[10] On the one hand, it makes cultivating tolerance easier, because it is supported by community laws, offices and civil servants. On the other, it considerably complicates the position of the liberal, as in spite of many variables and unknowns, he has to define both his tolerance and its limits. Obviously, it is not enough not to be an anti-Semite, religious fundamentalist or ethnic separatist. A liberal must also know who he should be in order not to disserve himself and others, and this as a rule turns out to be more difficult than in the times of monocultural societies.

2. Rational egoism

Both in the past and at present, this kind of egoism was not and is not as widely discussed and ostentatiously manifested as tolerance. This is perhaps a consequence of a variety of reasons. Suffice it to say that egoism itself generally evokes unfavourable associations and in many moral codes it is presented not as a virtue but rather as a manifestation of its lack. Nonetheless, no matter how one approaches such discretion, this kind of egoism was quite long ago clearly articulated and postulated already at the birth of liberalism, and when liberalism became a little more mature, egoism became one of its more important constituents. This is confirmed, for instance, by the *Declaration of the Rights of Man and of the Citizen* from 1789. As a matter of fact, it is not an exaggeration to claim that this is a declaration of a rational egoist and rational egoism.

Although the subsequent dramatic political events called into question many of the *Declaration*'s articles, its basis was not changed – it is, among others, rational egoism in its various forms. What is more, it has acquired the status of an international norm and has been registered as one of the most important declarations of the contemporary world, such as the Universal Declaration of Human Rights passed by the UN in 1948 or – also by the UN – the International Covenant on Civil and Political Rights from 1966. Rational egoism

[10] Cf. M. Walzer, *On Toleration*, New Haven – London 1997, p. 49.

also formed the basis of the plans and declarations which led to the establishment of the European Union, for example the plan by the French Minister of Foreign Affairs Robert Schumann (from 1950) or the Solemn Declaration of Stuttgart (from 1983).[11] Today, when this union is a fact and consists of most Western and Middle European countries, there is a search for such formulas which would allow optimally combining the egoisms of particular entities taking part within this great international enterprise. How difficult this task is was revealed, for example, during the discussions on the so-called European Constitution. In addition, the task's complexity is shown by the enormously voluminous size of the document.

The above battle had its original prelude in earlier treaties: from Maastricht (1991), Amsterdam (1997) and Nice (2001). Obviously, a common citizen is interested above all in the parts of these documents which could bring benefits to him. Thus, in the articles he can learn that he is given something as significant as "the right to work, live, settle down and use all social commodities in his place of residence everywhere in the EU, regardless of nationality." The fact that such rights find their place in the most important documents concerning Europe's present and future undoubtedly proves that the elites in authority are aware of the need to rise above individual and group egoisms. There is a lot of evidence, however, that common citizens in the countries of the so-called "old" European Union (which was made up of 15 countries) are afraid of such a "rising," which would mean that they will lose *their* jobs, *their* social benefits or *their* feeling of being at home. These fears lead to the situation in which the elites whose "to-be-or-not-to-be" on the political scene depends on the vote of each of those citizens begin a complicated process of playing for time (if this is a proper description of introducing the so-called transition periods for the realizations of these laws). One can of course laugh at French fears of a poorly qualified workforce from other countries, but arguably few so-called small shopkeepers are willing to laugh at the fears connected with the appearance in their native countries of the French trade giants. Obviously, such big companies do *their* own business. One can be doubtful, however, if they are doing it reasonably enough to consider their activities as being in accordance with the liberal moral code.

---

[11] The former was France's proposition for the countries destroyed in World War II to rise above mindless egoism of particular countries and together try to achieve economic revival and development; of special significance was the fact that the proposition was also addressed to Germany – the main author of the destruction and the traditional enemy of France. The Solemn Declaration of Stuttgart defines the main direction of European integration, such as the creation of supranational institutions, while at the same time preserving the Europe of Nations.

3. Calculated altruism

The above-mentioned example of big market chains operating in various European countries may be an interesting contribution to the discussion on contemporary altruism. In their branches, the client can make a relatively quick, cheap, comfortable purchase and occasional special offers and sales may create an impression that what actually happens there is not trade but the giving away of attractive products (for next to nothing). This kind of activity has, however, a second side to it. Typically, an average citizen does not hold any special interest in this activity, but what is said about it by the competition and written by specialists in the contemporary market gives food for thought with regard to the specific nature of this altruism. Generally speaking, big market chains operate within legally binding regulations. But from time to time their bosses forget that free market and free competition cannot mean protectionism, dumping, circumventing their workers' rights, etc., because in each case, someone has to pay for it. Usually, it turns out that the ones who pay are those who are economically weaker at this game.[12] Liberals have brought up the same issues for two centuries. Clearly, their moral code allows for both the calculation and accumulation of wealth, but it cannot take place at the cost of other people. When François Guizot exhorted people to "get rich," he certainly was not thinking about actions which would involve the maximum exploitation of a cheap workforce and the marginalization or total elimination of competition from the market.

Nevertheless, at first, the debate on calculated altruism concentrated not on economic issues, but on politics. It especially focused on the place and role of opposition. Before he took over high government positions, the same Guizot criticised those governments who think that "they will be self-sufficient," that is that they can rule while ignoring other social forces, including the opposition. Such behaviour is not only a sign of mindless egoism, but also devoid of any altruism whatsoever. The author of the treatise *On the Means of Government and Opposition in the Current State of France* contrasted this behaviour with the actions of those governments which not only see a place

---

[12] Adam Szymaniak attempted to prepare a synthesis of pros and cons of foreign market chains operating in Poland at the end of the 1990s – the results, however, are rather to their advantage. Cf. A. Szymaniak, "Zagraniczne sieci handlowe w Polsce w latach dziewięćdziesiątych" [Foreign Market Chains in Poland in the 1990s], in Z. Drozdowicz, Z.W. Puślecki (eds.), *Adaptacja przez transformacje* [Adaptation Through Transformations], Poznan 2001, p. 180 ff.

for political opposition in representative bodies, but also can use its presence for their specific benefits.[13]

Obviously, such behaviour of the authorities has little in common with Christian altruism, since the latter is about disinterestedness. In contrast, liberal altruism is about a calculated interestedness so that the ultimate balance of profits and losses should be to the advantage of the calculator, or at least so that he would not have to add too much to his altruism. Still, in the second half of the 19th century and at the beginning of the 20th, for many forces on the political scene, including liberals, it was not so much the preparation of the balance which was quite difficult, but putting it into practice.[14]

What does the situation look like today in the countries belonging to the European Union? Of course, one can find delegates of the ruling and opposing parties in their representative bodies. They are there not as a result of some kind of altruism, but thanks to the will and knowledge of those citizens who went to elections and voted for them out of duty or habit. However, one can notice a calculated altruism as early as at the stage of the creating of coalition parties. If an influential political party "clasps" a political "dwarf" to such a coalition and in addition gives it some governmental position, it is an act of specific altruism, but one having little in common with Christian mercy and more with political calculation. It does not matter if the "dwarf" is a liberal party or some other so-called low-importance political group. The readiness to form agreements and create coalitions of forces acting generally for the "common good," both promoted by liberals, have today become something of a standard political correctness.

A similar thing can be claimed about standards in culture. While one can criticize the bizarre inclinations of the youth, one cannot (under threat of becoming a laughing stock or being accused of stuffiness) forbid them to wear clothes which look like defective products or to use language which does not follow any dictionary rules of appropriate phrases. The situation of modern art is very similar. In order to establish whether something is a work of art or not, it is frequently not enough to use standard and non-standard criteria, and one has to entrust this matter to the artist himself or his fans. All this of course may be called the liberalization of contemporary life. But if one looks more closely at this process, it turns out that it would not be possible without

---

[13] "Opposition is there as a threatening and expectant force whose presence forces the government to exercise skill in their own system for fear of seeing the supporting forces abandon it and move under other banners." F. Guizot, *Des moyens de gouvernement et d'opposition dans l'état actuel de la France*, Bruxelles 1846, p. 206.

[14] This is noted by, for example, Émile Faguet. Cf. É. Faguet, *Liberalizm* [Liberalism], Lvov s.a. (especially the chapter "O prawie mniejszości" [On the Right of Minority]).

tolerance, rational egoism and calculated altruism. Obviously, the order does not always have to be the same. However, the slogan of freedom has to be invariably in the first place. Without it, one cannot talk about liberalism at all.

4. Responsibility

Clearly enough, responsibility is required not only of liberals, and even not only of the representatives of political groups, but of everyone who participates in social life and influences the lives of others. Liberals were aware of this, although they did not always confirm it through their actions in society. To justify them, one may at least say that they learned responsibility not within the walls of an esteemed university where everything is already regulated and follows its own usually leisurely pace, but during abridged "courses" on social life, that is, while being entangled in current affairs – sometimes co-authoring them and sometimes surrendering to the development of events which could not have been foreseen nor even controlled.

They received a particularly severe lesson at the end of the 18th century and in the first half of the 19th century. But as a matter of fact, this was when they reached their maturity, transforming themselves from politicizing philosophers, lawyers and historians into professional political leaders, as it became their privilege to govern and participate in governing. For them, it meant not only a special social advancement, but also a test of truth – in confrontation with the reality of social life – including of all their slogans, postulates and social programmes. It is debatable whether they revealed themselves to be such bright students in this school of life as to award them a positive mark. Perhaps their opponents will maintain that they learned little and are still saying generally the same things which are written in various declarations of human and citizen rights. But even their opponents have to admit that in this case, "generally the same" does not mean that there have appeared no important disambiguations, supplements and corrections.

I do not want to go into details at this point. It must be recalled, however, that at the beginning of their presence in public life as well as now, they have combined responsibility not only with what is being said but what is, was and should be done. There is a lot to prove that for a liberal a responsible person is someone who not only refrains from speaking out socially dangerous slogans and postulates, but also objects to others doing so. It is especially noticeable during electoral campaigns for various representative assemblies. As of today, it is a truly festive period for populists, revanchists and various kinds of social "charlatans." What it looks like in practice is observable on the political scene, both in the so-called "old" and young democracies (such as the one in Poland).

Obviously, in order to talk about responsibility in accordance with liberal standards, it is not enough to speak responsibly and oppose others' irresponsible pronouncements, but also to act responsibly: in various fields and to various extents. This is usually much more complex and challenging than first thought. The mere attempt to define responsible action poses considerable difficulties. Therefore, let us put it in a nutshell:

– in terms of political activities, responsible action for a liberal should mean that he will discuss and try to convince everyone of his views and plans, regardless of their denomination, political affiliation or other preferences;

– in terms of economic activity, he should be – in fact, as well as others – focused on gaining profit, but in contrast to others he should take care of such a division of profits that what he earns is a natural outcome of his work;

– in terms of everyday behaviour, responsible action means demonstrating at every moment his doubts as to tastes, inclinations or convictions of his nearer or farther surroundings; for instance, he should not change the TV channel as soon as on the screen he can see – in his opinion an obnoxious (but for his close ones interesting and moving) – a soap opera; not to mention the appearance of the political opponents whose comments make him grit his teeth.

The above is of course a bit jocular, but in my opinion it is not completely irrelevant. I believe liberals would agree with me that the so-called forging of liberal virtues begins at the bottom and not at the top of living and co-existing with others, including one's closest environment.

5. Predictability

Predictability is not always a virtue. It is relatively easy to imagine a situation in which it is a sign of recklessness or simple stupidity; for instance, in such a political game where it is better to keep in secret from our opponents what we are going to bet on or how we are going to act. It is, however, a virtue when in general it is not concerned with any games, tricks or securing particular interests (individual and group ones), but with the common good of those with whom we live and co-exist and even whose fate we sometimes have in our hands. Such a positioning of this virtue may become many people's privilege. In any case, it is a privilege which does not belong exclusively to those who follow liberal ideology. In my view, liberals are those who should employ this virtue more frequently. It goes without saying that they spoke, speak and probably will still speak about freedom. It can even be considered their "trademark." The problem is, however, that people began talking about freedom long before liberals appeared in this imperfect world and made an attempt to improve it.

Actually, liberals quite early expressed their *votum separatum* at some of these ways of understanding and realizing freedom. Unfortunately, it was not effective enough to prevent people from mistaking liberalism with, for example, the ethical codes of medieval corporations or the slogans of today's separatist movements. In short, in order to be able to talk about liberal predictability, a liberal has to say and do more than just declare a few slogans and make a few ideological statements. Of course, liberals have always been aware of this. Among others, this is confirmed by numerous and often voluminous treatises where the most frequently repeated and inflected word is *liberalism*. For outsiders observing the liberals' struggle, it constitutes more of a problem of abundance rather than of scarcity. This is because it is often hard to understand to which point liberals proceed on a common front and where their paths begin to diverge, generating further liberal factions. Nonetheless, it is possible to point to what they together will with some consistency be steadfast about. The above thoughts contain an attempt to delineate those minima without which it is impossible to talk about liberalism as a significant social ideology. Therefore, I will merely add here that there is not and cannot be any liberalism without believing in human beings: in their natural and acquired abilities, in their power to transform reality in such a way that today can be better than yesterday and tomorrow better than today. Obviously, this faith has little in common with religions, where God is in the first place. But it is also not connected with a so-called "blind" faith, meaning the faith which relies on fortunate coincidence. From the liberal point of view, if one does not help oneself, no one and nothing will help, and counting on the help from any *force majeure* is at least fallible and carries with it the risk of great failure. It is perhaps the most fundamental of liberal moral messages.

Annex

Liberalism in Poland after communism

I would like to return once more to Jerzy Szacki's book *Liberalizm po komunizmie* [Liberalism after Communism]. In it, Szacki presents an in-depth analysis of the state of liberalism and its social reception in the so-called post-communist countries of Eastern Europe, one of which is Poland. In 1989, it freed itself from the corset of communism and started to frantically search for a "suit" in which it would feel most comfortable or at least which would have the best "look." There is a certain amount of sarcasm in this, but for a reason. This is because the actions undertaken in East European countries in this respect are suggestive of the behaviour of someone who became part of the so-called good company but as yet has not mastered its manners nor is aware of which ones should and which should not be imitated. Such a comparison is not taken from Szacki's book. It corresponds, however, with its descriptions of the clashes of various ideologies in such countries as Hungary, the Czech Republic and Poland. One of the main protagonists of these battles (actually, not always positive ones) is liberalism.

In the introduction, Szacki already notes that "in Eastern Europe, it is surprising how many people admit to following liberalism, sometimes even in such a 'pure' form which would probably be forgotten in the West if it were not for the heroic efforts of a handful of theoreticians who rarely met with understanding from the practitioners and the majority of university colleagues."[1] A bit further he observes that "in the eyes of the growing number of supporters and even of people who would not define themselves as such, liberalism is not only one of many orientations which sprang up so abundantly on the

[1] Cf. J. Szacki, *Liberalizm po komunizmie* [Liberalism after Communism], Cracow 1994, p. 6 ff.

ruins of the old order, but something more: a heralding of a new society which should be built as quickly as possible or, in any case, the determination of its absolutely necessary foundations, where entering into discussion about other solutions is in a sense pointless." Szacki confirms his view with the help of the opinion of Janusz Lewandowski ("one of the leading theoreticians and practitioners of Polish liberalism," a co-founder of the political party called the Liberal Democratic Congress).

At this point there emerges a problem with liberalism in general, with Polish liberalism and with liberalism in Poland in particular. It is not about the fact that in the past as well as today there was and still is more than one liberalism, and also not because it is impossible to formulate one convincing definition of liberalism (J. Szacki points this out in part II of his book). The point is that the path leading to the liberalisms which we encounter today in Western countries was long and hard. These liberalisms had to wage victorious battles with various opponents at different stages of their acquiring the right of citizenship and social acceptance. This, however, was not enough to achieve the social successes which became their privilege in the 19th and 20th centuries. They also had to count on favourable social conditions, such as the changing structure of Western societies (with urban communities gaining an increasingly stronger position within them) or the development of the economy (with industry and commerce coming to the fore). All this constituted a stark contrast to "the reality of backward East-European societies with their half-feudal socio-economic structure, sparse and weak middle class and the majority of illiterate peasantry who in the times of B. Constant or J. S. Mill were going through serfdom and to a large extent remained within the natural economy." This prevented liberalism in this part of Europe from growing into an ideological and political power.[2]

The communist period in Poland and other East European countries was also hard for liberalism. This was because it was fought both by communist theory and by practical actions of the ruling communists; it was so zealously attacked because it was perceived as the most serious threat to communism – "the only advocate of progress." J. Szacki draws attention to the appearance of a peculiar paradox at that time in this part of Europe – "the opposition of communism and liberalism in real social countries was a circumstance conducive to the survival of some liberal ideas as well as to their reception and, as it were, to their independent discovery." The mouthpiece for these ideas at that time were most of all democratic opposition groups, such as, at first, Komitet Obrony Robotników [The Workers' Defence Committee] and later "Solidar-

[2] Cf. ibidem, p. 62 ff.

ity" in Poland. Everything that took place in Poland after the breakthrough in 1989, including the pros and cons of the reform by the then deputy prime minister and the minister of finance Leszek Balcerowicz, as well as the political successes and failures of Kongres Liberalny [The Liberal Congress] and Unia Wolności [The Freedom Union], are explained by Szacki both as a result of social expectations and significant restrictions that liberals faced in Poland.

With such fragile traditions of Polish liberal thought and such serious difficulties in getting through to society's consciousness and social practice, the contemporary state of liberalism in Poland cannot be satisfactory. The problem is, however, that it has to be better than it is now. It results not from the wishes of Polish liberals but from the necessity to meet those objectives and challenges which are a consequence of Polish membership in the European Union. It is because the leading positions there belong to those countries where liberalism has become the constituent not only of politics but also of everyday social practice and where there is no need to put too much effort into explaining basic liberal principles to common citizens. In Poland, a number of those liberal principles requires explanation, and it still happens that influential politicians and influential social groups think and talk about their rights (understood as "entitlements to...") as if not much has changed since the times of the Polish democracy of the nobles.

I am not the only one expressing such an evaluation of the condition of liberalism in today's Poland. A similar opinion can be found in Marcin Król's book *Liberalizm strachu czy liberalizm odwagi* [The Liberalism of Fear or the Liberalism of Courage]. Król claims that in every case, the components of liberalism are both fear and hope, but in the Polish reality it is rather the former that takes precedence. According to him, this is confirmed by the "scathing remarks" of those Polish liberals who before the breakthrough of 1989 "were afraid that solidarity-moralistic endeavours will in the future hamper the radical introduction of free market mechanisms and the rule of the law. In fact, they thought that the free market and the rule of law are in a progressive country a sufficient basis for pursuing politics, and the formulation of social and political objectives in other categories may merely disrupt the clarity and effectiveness of this – in their view – modern and Western programme."[3]

The list of those anxieties, fears and concerns is of course longer. Among the most important ones, Król recognizes the fear of: 1) the demarcation by liberalism of "The Maginot Line" between the advocates of "positive freedom" ("in particular, referring to control over one's personal life") and "negative

[3] M. Król, *Liberalizm strachu czy liberalizm odwagi* [Liberalism of Fear or Liberalism of Courage], Cracow – Warsaw 1996.

freedom" (understood as independence from something or someone and "an ability to perceive the world simply as either black or white"); and 2) nationalism and religious fundamentalism. Król writes about the former that "in some way it is xenophobic, it limits the freedom of those not belonging to the nation," while the latter is perceived and presented as "a threat to the liberal perception of the world and to the institution of liberal democracy. It is not about members of a given religious community being convinced that their faith and truth are the only legitimate ones, but about their conviction being transferred to public life and forcing others to accept their truth without objections and outside usual democratic procedures."[4]

The fear of nationalism and religious fundamentalism inspired by liberals gives rise to similar reactions on the other side of this peculiar social barricade, meaning the inspiration of the fear of liberalism not only in Poland but actually in all those countries which struggled to fashion their national identity and which still remember the hardships on their way to achieving this goal. Thus, is there in Europe at least one country where these processes went easily and peacefully and where influential social groups have forgotten the traumas of these ordeals? Even in the countries which can reasonably claim to be considered and presented as thosee countries with open borders to foreigners there is a considerable acceptance and political support for such slogans as: "France for the French," "Germany for Germans," "England for Englishmen," etc. And these are merely signals of internal tensions and conflicts which put into question such liberal virtues as tolerance or the ability to rise above racial and cultural differences.

In today's Poland, there are no longer such numerous cultural and religious minorities as before World War II, but still slogans like "Poland for Poles" or "Pole-Catholic" come to light and not in every case may they be said to represent a special kind of folklore. Obviously, these days, the list of enemies of those considering themselves "real Poles" is different from the list used by the pre-war National Democracy.[5] On both of these lists, however, significant places belong to liberals or at least those who were called *liberals*. "Real Poles" have been giving this name to all those who, for various reasons,

[4] Ibidem, p. 37.

[5] This was a political group which, at the end of the 19th century and in the first half of the 20th promoted the slogans of Polish independence, social solidarity of Poles, nationalism, anti-Semitism and antisocialism. In 1918–1939, it was led by Roman Dmowski, among other things the author of political ideology pamphlets *Nasz patriotyzm* [Our Patriotism] and *Myśli nowoczesnego Polaka* [The Thoughts of the Modern Pole]. Today in Poland his ideology is referred to by such political parties as Liga Rodzin Polskich [The League of Polish Families] as well as youth organizations, for instance Młodzież Wszechpolska [The Nationwide Polish Youth].

isolate themselves from the Catholic religion and Catholic religiousness, which of course does not yet mean that they identify themselves with liberal ideology or liberal social philosophy. It must be emphasised that arguments for using the term *liberalism* so freely have been supplied by those politicians who have a limited understanding of what liberalism was, is and can be, but still use slogans which were borrowed from liberals, for example "free market" or "the separation of Church and state." In the 1990s, such slogans were used by Unia Polityki Realnej [The Real Politics Union] and today it is used by Ruch Poparcia Palikota [The Movement of Support for Palikot]. These parties do not enjoy widespread social approval. However, the postulates put forward by their leaders (for instance: privatization of everything that can be privatized or maximising the marginalization of the Church's role in public life) not only supply the opponents of liberalism with arguments against it but also to ridicule liberalism as a serious and in many respects courageous social philosophy. They also force those who either identify with liberalism or at least sympathize with it to explain that liberalism is not the proverbial "camel," that is, it does not need to have those "humps" usually ascribed to it by its opponents and professed supporters.

Such explanations appear, for example, in Marcin Król's book. He states, for instance, that the separation of the Church and state postulated by liberals "cannot certainly be achieved by turning Churches into interest groups or voluntary associations. This is because Churches differ from swimming or reading societies in the respect [...] that they preach the truth. And it is this truth that causes so many problems for us." Król also explains what these "problems" are and points out the ways in which liberals could cope with them (in his opinion, "it requires of liberalism a certain amount of good will to acknowledge the reality of faith, similarly to the acknowledgment of the reality of nationalism").

However, it must be clearly stated that Marcin Król's liberal discussion on and about liberalism in Poland and other countries is located at such a high intellectual level of thinking and talking about liberalism that it probably will not be of interest to the so-called average Pole. It is easier to reach him or her with messages from those who associate liberalism with specific people (for example, Leszek Balcerowicz), plans (for example, "the Balcerowicz plan") and specific results of their realization (for example, the total collapse of Państwowe Gospodarstwa Rolne [National Farmsteads]).

The claim that thanks to these people, their plans and achievement, Poland is not only more liberal but also more frugal or normal (by West-European standards of normality) is of course good news. It is good news, however, for those who benefit from this normality. It is bad news for those who, thanks to it, lost their meagre, but nevertheless steady jobs, steady incomes, steady opportunities to use a range of welfare benefits or simply their basis for social functioning according to the rules of various minima and minimalisms. I only want to say that neither in the past nor now is liberalism for those who are ready be satisfied with those minima and minimalisms. This refers not only to Poland but also to those countries where liberalism already has a strong social position.

Bibliography

Adorno F. M., Gregory T., Verra V., *Storia della filosofia*, vol. 3, Roma – Bari 1977.

Aristotle, *Etyka nikomachejska* [Nicomachean Ethics], Wydawnictwo Naukowe PWN, Warsaw 2000.

Aron R., *Démocratie et totalitarisme*, Eddition Galimard, Paris 1965.

Aron R., *Widz i uczestnik* [Observer and Participant], Czytelnik, Warsaw 1992.

Banach W., *Spontaniczność a planowanie. Wokół filozofii społecznej Friedricha A. von Hayeka* [Spontaneity and Planning. About the Social Philosophy of Friedrich A. von Hayek], Wydawnictwo Fundacji Humaniora, Poznan 2003.

Banaszak M. Fr., *Historia Kościoła katolickiego* [The History of the Catholic Church], vol. 3, ATK, Warsaw 1991.

Baszkiewicz J., *Historia Francji* [The History of France], Ossolineum, Wroclaw – Warsaw – Cracow 2004.

Beccaria C., *Dei delitti e delle pene*, Unione Tipografico-Editrice Torinese, Torino 1911.

Bentham J., *An Introduction to the Principles of Morality and Legislation*, Clarendon Press, Oxford 1909.

Berlin I., *Four Essays on Liberty*, Oxford University Press, London 1969.

Bocheński J. M., *Lewica, religia, sowietologia* [The Left, Religion, Sovietology], Morex, Warsaw 1996.

Chateaubriand R., *De la Monarchie selon la charte*, Le Normant, Paris 1816.

Condorcet A. N., *Szkic obrazu postępu ducha ludzkiego poprzez dzieje* [Sketch for a Historical Picture of the Progress of the Human Mind], PWN, Warsaw.

Courtois S. et al., *The Black Book of Communism: Crimes, Terror, Repression. Collective Works*, Harvard University Press, Cambridge – London 1999.

Coxe W., *Travels into Poland, Russia, Sweden, and Denmark: Interspersed with Historical Relations and Political Inquiries*, vol. 1, printed by J. Nichols, for T. Cadell, London 1784.

Croce B., *Aspetti morali della vita politica*, Napoli 1927; reprint: *Elementi di politica*, Laterza, Bari 1966.

Cuoco V., *Saggio storico sulla rivoluzione napoletana del 1799*, d'Ajala 1861.

Cuoco V., *Scritti vari di V.C.*, Bari 1924.

d'Holbach P. T., *Etokracja czyli rząd oparty na moralności* [Ethocracy or Government Founded on Ethics], PWN, Warsaw 1979.

Faguet É., *Kult niekompetencji* [The Cult of Incompetence], Polskie Towarzystwo Pedagogiczne, Lvov – Warsaw 1922.

Faguet É., *Le Libéralisme*, Soc. Fr. d'Imprimerie et de Librairie, Paris 1902.

Faguet É., *Liberalizm* [Liberalism], Lvov s.a.

Fauré Ch. (ed.), *Les déclaration des droits de l'homme de 1789. Textes réunis et présentés par Christine Fauré*, Editions Payot, Paris 1988.

Fejtö F., *Histoire des démocraties populaires*, vol. 1, Seuil, Paris 1979.

Gramsci A., *Il materialismo storico e la filosofia di Benedetto Croce*, Einaudi, Torino 1948.

Gray J., *Liberalizm* [Liberalism], Znak, Cracow 1994.

Gray J., *Liberalisms. Essays in Political Philosophy*, Routledge, New York 1989.

Guizot F., *Des moyens de gouvernement et d'opposition dans l'état actuel de la France*, Bruxelles 1846.

Hallowell J. H., *The Moral Foundation of Democracy*, University of Chicago Press, Chicago 1954.

Hayek F. A., *Law, Legislation and Liberty*, University of Chicago Press, Chicago 1973.

Hayek F. A., *The Constitution of Liberty*, The University of Chicago Press, Chicago 1978.

Hayek F. A., *The Road to Serfdom*, Routledge, London 2006.

Hazard P., *Myśl europejska w XVIII wieku. Od Monteskiusza do Lessinga* [European Thought in the Eighteenth Century. From Montesquieu to Lessing], PIW, Warsaw 1972.

Hegel G. W. F., "Philosophische Propädeutik," in idem, *Sämtliche Werke. Jubiläumsausgabe in zwanzig Bänden*, vol. 3, ed. H. Glockner, Stuttgart 1927–1940.

Hegel G. W. F., *Philosophy of Right*, Batoche Books, Kitchener 2001.

Heller M., Niekricz A., *Utopia u władzy. Historia Związku Sowieckiego* [Utopia in Power. The History of the Soviet Union], vol. 1, Universitas, Wroclaw 1989.

Herzog D., *Happy Slaves: A Critique of Consent Theory*, University of Chicago Press, Chicago 1989.

Hobhouse L., *Liberalism*, Oxford University Press, London 1945.

Humboldt W. von, *Über die Grenzen der Wirksamkeit des Staates* [On the Limits of State Action], Verlag Hans Carl, Nuremberg 1946.

Jellinek G., *Die Erklärung der Menschen- und Bürgerrechte*, 2nd ed., Leipzig 1904.

Jones G. S., Patterson I. (eds.), *Fourier: The Theory of the Four Movements*, Cambridge University Press, Cambridge 1996.

Kaczocha W., *Demokracja proceduralna oraz republikańska* [Procedural and Republican Democracy], AE, Poznan 2004.

Kant I., "Co to jest Oświecenie?" [Was ist Aufklärung?], in T. Kroński, *Kant*, Wiedza Powszechna, Warsaw 1966.

Kasprzyk L., *Spencer*, Wiedza Powszechna, Warsaw 1967.

Kołakowski L., *Main Currents of Marxism: Its Rise, Growth, and Dissolution*, vol. 2, Clarendon Press, London 1978.

Kołłątaj H., *Wybór pism naukowych* [Selected Scientific Papers], PWN, Warsaw 1953.

Krasuski J., *Historia Niemiec* [The History of Germany], Ossolineum, Wroclaw – Warsaw – Cracow 2004.

Kroński T., *Kant*, Wiedza Powszechna, Warsaw 1966.

Król M., *Liberalizm strachu czy liberalizm odwagi* [Liberalism of Fear or Liberalism of Courage], Znak – Fundacja im. Stefana Batorego, Cracow – Warsaw 1996.

Kuderowicz Z., *Hegel i jego uczniowie* [*Hegel and His Disciples*], Wiedza Powszechna, Warsaw 1984.
Lamennais H.-F.-R. de, *Słowa wierzącego* [Words of a Believer], in idem, *Wybór pism* [Select Writings], Książka i Wiedza, Warsaw 1970.
Locke J., *A Letter Concerning Toleration*, W. Otrige, London 1812.
Locke J., *Two Treaties of Government*, New American Library, New York 1963.
Macedo S., *Cnoty liberalne* [Liberal Virtues. Citizenship, Virtue and Community], Znak, Cracow 1995.
Macedo S., *Liberal Virtues. Citizenship, Virtue and Community*, Oxford University Press, Oxford 1990.
Maistre J. de, *Considérations sur la France. Oeuvres Complets*, vol. I, Paris 1940.
Maistre J. de, *Des Constitutions politiques et des autres institutions humaines*, Strasbourg 1959.
Maistre J. de, *Les Soirées de Saint-Pétersbourg ou Entretiens sur le gouvernement temporel de la Providence*, Paris 1821.
Malthus T. R., *An Essay on the Principle of Population*, Cambridge University Press, Cambridge 1992.
Manent P., *An Intellectual History of Liberalism*, Princeton University Press, Princeton, New Jersey 1995.
Mannheim K., *Ideology and Utopia. An Introduction to the Sociology of Knowledge*, Routledge and Kegan Paul, London 1954.
Mannheim K., *Myśl konserwatywna* [Conservative Thought], Kolegium Otryckie, Warsaw 1986.
Mill J. S., *Considerations on Representative Government*, Parker, Son, and Bourn, London 1861.
Mill J. S., *On Liberty*, Longman, Green and Co., London 1867.
Mill J. S., *Utilitarianism*, Longmans, Green, and Co., London 1879.
Montesquieu, *Listy perskie* [Persian Letters], Książka i Wiedza, Warsaw 1951.
Montesquieu, *The Spirit of the Laws*, Cambridge University Press, Cambridge 2006.
Natali G., *Cultura e poesia in Italia nell'età napoleonica*, Sten, Torino 1930.
Naumann F., *Das Prinzip des Liberalismus*, in idem, *Die Politik der Gegenwart*, Berlin 1905.
Nozick R., *Anarchy, State, and Utopia*, Blackwell, Malden, Oxford 1991.
Popper K. R., *Conjectures and Refutations*, Routledge, London 2002.
Popper K. R., *Open Society and Its Enemies*, Princeton University Press, Princeton 1950.
Procacci G., *Historia Włochów* [The History of the Italian People], PWN, Warsaw 1983.
Putnam D., *Making Democracy Work: Civic Traditions in Modern Italy*, Princeton, Princeton University Press.
Ranke L., *Dzieje papiestwa w XVI–XIX wieku* [The History of the Papacy from the XVI to the XIX Centuries], vol. 1, PIW, Warsaw 1974.
Rau Z., *Liberalizm. Zarys myśli politycznej XIX i XX wieku* [Liberalism. An Outline of Political Thought in the XIX and XX Centuries], Fundacja Aletheia, Warsaw 2000.
Rawls J., *A Theory of Justice*, Belknap Press of Harvard University Press, Cambridge 1999.
Ricardo D., *The Principles of Political Economy and Taxation*, John Murray, Albemarle-Street, London 1821.
Ruggiero de G., *The History of European Liberalism*, Beacon Press, Boston 1959.
Sartori G., *Democratic Theory*, Wayne State University Press, Detroit 1962.

Seidler G. L., *W nurcie filozofii Oświecenia* [In the Mainstream of the Enlightenment], Wydawnictwo Lubelskie, Lublin 1984.

Self P., *Political Theories of Moderns Government*, Allen and Unwin, London 1985.

Sikora A., *Lamennais czyli dramat konsekwencji*, Wstęp [Introduction] in H. -F. -R. de Lamennais, *Wybór pism* [Lamennais or the Drama of the Consequences, Introduction to: H.- F.- R. de Lamennais, Select Writings], Książka i Wiedza, Warsaw 1970.

Smith A., *Inquiry into the Nature and Causes of the Wealth of Nations*, W. Strahan and T. Cadell, London 1776.

Sobolewska B., Sobolewski M. (eds.), *Myśl polityczna XIX i XX w. Liberalizm* [Political Thought of 19th and 20th Century Liberalism], PWN, Warsaw 1978.

Spencer H., *First Principles*, Watts, London 1945.

Spencer H., *Progress, its Laws and Causes*, in idem, *Essays, Scientific, Political and Speculative*, vol. 3, Williams and Norgate, London 1891.

Spencer H., *Social Statics,* John Chapman, London 1902.

Staszic S., *Pisma filozoficzne i społeczne*, t. I [Philosophical and Social Writings, vol. 1], PWN, Warsaw 1954.

Stein L. von, *Socialismus und Communismus des heutigen Frankkreichs*, Leipzig 1848.

Szacki J., *Kontrrewolucyjne paradoksy. Wizje świata francuskich antagonistów Wielkiej Rewolucji 1789–1815* [Counterrevolutionary Paradoxes. The French Antagonists of the Great 1789–1815 Revolution and Their Visions of the World], PWN, Warsaw 1965

Szacki J., *Liberalizm po komunizmie* [Liberalism after Communism], Znak, Cracow 1994.

Szymaniak A., "Zagraniczne sieci handlowe w Polsce w latach dziewięćdziesiątych" [Foreign Market Chains in Poland in the 1990's], in Z. Drozdowicz, Z.W. Puślecki (eds.), *Adaptacja przez transformacje*, [Adaptation Through Transformations], Wydawnictwo Fundacji Humaniora, Poznan 2001.

Thiers L. A., *La Monarchie de 1830*, Paris 1831.

Titone V., *La storiografia dell'illuminismo in Iltalia*, Mursia, Milano 1969.

Tocqueville A. de, *Democracy in America*, vol. I, University of Chicago Press, Chicago 2000.

Voltaire, *Letters Concerning the English Nation*, J. and R. Tonson, D. Midwinter, M. Cooper, and J. Hodges, London 1778.

Walzer M., *On Toleration*, Yale University Press, New Haven – London 1997.

Wolter [Voltaire], *Traktat o tolerancji napisany z powodu śmierci Jana Calasa* [Treatise on Tolerance On the Occasion of the Death of Jean Calas], PIW, Warsaw 1956.

Zins H., *Historia Anglii* [The History of England], Ossolineum, Wroclaw – Warsaw – Cracow 2001.

Index of persons

* References to footnotes are in italics.

Andrzej Przyłebski
Sense, Meaning and Understanding
Towards a Systematic Hermeneutical Philosophy
vol. 9, 2013, ca. 160 pp., ca. 29,90 €, br., ISBN-CH 978-3-643-90378-5